BARNSTORMERS & SPEED KINGS

*This volume is one of a series that traces the adventure and
science of aviation, from the earliest manned balloon ascension
through the era of jet flight.*

BARNSTORMERS & SPEED KINGS

by Paul O'Neil

AND THE EDITORS OF TIME-LIFE BOOKS

TIME-LIFE BOOKS, ALEXANDRIA, VIRGINIA

THE AUTHOR
Paul O'Neil began his career as a newspaper-
man and short-story writer in Seattle, where
he grew up. In 1944 he moved to New York
and worked for *Time, Sports Illustrated* and
Life until he became a freelance writer in
1973. He is the author of three volumes in the
Time-Life Books series The Old West.

THE CONSULTANT
for *Barnstormers & Speed Kings*
Walter J. Boyne is Assistant Director of the
National Air and Space Museum in Washington. A retired United States Air Force colonel
and command pilot, Boyne has written several books and nearly 200 articles on various
aviation subjects.

THE CONSULTANTS *for The Epic of Flight*
Melvin B. Zisfein, the principal consultant, is
Deputy Director of the National Air and
Space Museum, Washington. He received
degrees in aeronautical engineering from the
Massachusetts Institute of Technology and
has contributed to many scientific, techno-
logical and historical publications. He is an
Associate Fellow of the American Institute of
Aeronautics and Astronautics.

Charles Harvard Gibbs-Smith, Research Fellow at the Science Museum, London, and
a Keeper-Emeritus of the Victoria and Al-
bert Museum, London, has written or edited
some 20 books and numerous articles on
aeronautical history. In 1978 he served as the
first Lindbergh Professor of Aerospace History at the National Air and Space Museum,
Smithsonian Institution, Washington.

Dr. Hidemasa Kimura, honorary professor at
Nippon University, Tokyo, is the author of
numerous books on the history of aviation
and is a widely known authority on aeronautical engineering and aircraft design. One
plane that he designed established a world
distance record in 1938.

Library of Congress Cataloguing in Publication Data
O'Neil, Paul, 1909.
    Barnstormers & speed kings.
    (The Epic of flight)
    Bibliography: p.
    Includes index.
    1. Aeronautical sports — History. I. Time-Life Books.
II. Title. III. Series: Epic of flight.
GV753.O53   797.5'4   80-13736
ISBN 0-8094-3277-3
ISBN 0-8094-3276-5 lib. bdg.
ISBN 0-8094-3275-7 retail ed.

CONTENTS

Sure-footed showmen of the sky

They were a surplus commodity of the Great War: out-of-work aviators flying out-of-work airplanes, and during the restless years following that war they found a unique and satisfying way to survive, as itinerant showmen of the air. The barnstormers, as they called themselves, were a largely American phenomenon, wandering from coast to coast to perform in rough pastures, at big-city air shows and, when fortune beckoned, in motion-picture melodramas.

At first, these gypsy fliers could keep their stomachs and fuel tanks full by merely offering rides—for five dollars and up—in their Curtiss Jennys. Then, as novelty wore thin, the barnstormers teamed up to develop repertoires of spectacular tricks. They walked on the wings and attempted increasingly reckless acrobatics in mid-air: changing planes or transferring from a speeding automobile, train or boat. They recruited young women daredevils to increase the lure and heighten the excitement. And before their show had run its course, they had introduced a hesitant public to the thrills of flight.

In an attempt to transfer from a speeding car to a plane on the beach near San Diego in 1920, Clyde Pangborn grips a specially installed bar on a Lozier automobile (below), then reaches for the ladder dangling from partner Ralph Reed's approaching Jenny (bottom left). Yanked skyward (top right), Pangborn loses his grip and falls toward a bone-jarring landing on the sand.

Pilot Ron MacDougall steadies the wings as his teammates Spider Matlock (left) and Fronty Nichols reach for a pair of doffed hats in 1924.

piloted by his partner, Milton "Skeets" Elliott. In this sequence
he stands upside down (below) and spread-eagled on the top wing
(bottom), then hangs by his boots from the lower wing (right).

Gladys Ingle's mid-air change of planes is recorded in this sequence by photographers in both planes. Below, poised on the upper wing of one Jenny, she waits for the second plane to approach. As it draws closer (bottom) she prepares to grab a strut and then (right) hoists herself onto the lower wing.

No ball is in play in this mock tennis match, but a simple overswing could mean a fatal fall for wingwalker Gladys Roy (top) or Ivan Unger.

1

An invasion of freewheeling gypsies

Lincoln Beachey, greatest of early American aviators, was born into a world yet without wings. But he believed he was born to fly and that when the time came, he would know exactly how to do it. By 1910, at the age of 23, he had built and operated his own dirigible and felt qualified to offer his services to the pioneer aircraft builder Glenn Curtiss, who hoped to interest Americans in aviation with his touring exhibition fliers. Curtiss agreed to allow Beachey to audition. The brash young man, possessor of a monumental ego and an ugly temper, refused to accept the most rudimentary flight instruction after seating himself in one of Curtiss' planes and crashed repeatedly before learning to control it. In the air, however, he demonstrated an intuitive sense of maneuver and an almost unbelievable ability to compensate for the imperfections of the aircraft of the day.

He soon managed to improve the airplane itself. Many early designers believed, with the Wright brothers, that planes needed two sets of elevators, fore and aft. Curtiss' planes boasted a pair of elevators, mounted ahead of wings and engine on a long, spindly boom, to augment a similar set at the tail. At an exhibition shortly after he joined the Curtiss team in 1911, Beachey tore off the front boom in a collision with a fence. He insisted on taking to the air anyway, and not only lived—to the astonishment of Curtiss' mechanics—but flew so well that other aviators soon began dispensing with the front boom.

He lusted to exceed the world altitude record, which then stood at 10,466 feet, but was assured that his Curtiss pusher plane was incapable of climbing to such a height—a conclusion based on the machine's fuel capacity of seven gallons and on the widely held assumption that a pilot needed fuel for his descent. Beachey simply strapped a 10-gallon tank on his plane, climbed until it was empty, and—having reached a new record altitude of 11,642 feet—glided to earth with a dead engine.

But it was Beachey's hair-raising ability to fly in and out of little ball parks and to zip under telephone wires and the branches of trees that endeared him to audiences and made him unique. He dressed for flying in a pin-striped suit, high starched collar, tie with diamond stickpin and a golfing cap worn backward—and made a practice of tearing past grandstands just a foot or so off the ground with the steering lever gripped between his knees and both arms flung wide to thrill the crowds.

He provided his most memorable thrill—to a crowd of 150,000— when he flew over the edge of Niagara Falls, dived steeply into the mists

Cap spun backward, chin firmly set, Lincoln Beachey grips the wheel of his Curtiss pusher in 1912 with the determination that made him the most daring flier of his day—and the prototype of a generation of post-World War I barnstormers.

below, pulled up just above the whirlpools that seemed about to swallow his plane, tore on downstream and under an obstructing bridge, zoomed up and over cliffs on the Canadian side and finally landed, dripping wet but safe and sound, on a field to the west of the river.

Beachey retired at the end of 1912, in part because he had come to believe the public only wanted to see him kill himself, and in part because newspapers had begun blaming him for the deaths of aviators who tried to imitate him. But he could not bear to be outdone and returned to the air on hearing that a Frenchman named Adolphe Pégoud had performed in September 1913 a stunt thought impossible— pulling his Blériot monoplane up in a climbing arc until he was upside down, then diving to close a complete circle called a loop.

Beachey looped a Curtiss biplane not once but three times in succession only two months later in the skies over Coronado, California, and capped this exploit by taking off, flying about and landing inside the Machinery Palace, a cavernous exhibition hall that had been built for the upcoming Panama-Pacific Exposition in San Francisco.

He set his chief mechanic, Warren Eaton, to work in San Francisco, meanwhile, building a sleek monoplane with a tricycle landing gear— with which he promised to entertain crowds at the exposition. He had the machine dismantled and stored after a series of test flights, however, and flew his regular aircraft during the first three weeks of the fair. It was rumored that he had discovered flaws in the new plane, and when he finally agreed—at the insistence of officials at the fair—to fly it in a performance on Sunday, March 14, 1915, he drew a crowd of 50,000.

Beachey climbed 6,000 feet into the sunshine over San Francisco Bay and began his most difficult stunt: a vertical S that he performed by putting his plane into the first 180 degrees of an outside loop, flying upside down, and then nosing over into an inside loop to complete the outline of the letter S in the sky. But something went wrong as he tried to pull out of his final dive. His vertical speed passed the aircraft's design limit of 103 miles per hour and, according to estimates made during a later investigation, had reached almost 200 when the wings folded back and collapsed; the plane raised a fountain of water as it plummeted into the Bay, its engine's howl quenched in sudden silence as it disappeared.

A diver from the battleship *Oregon* was hurriedly dispatched to locate the wreck; all involved worked as frantically as if they believed the flier might still be alive. Only 35 minutes passed before the remains of the monoplane were drawn up from the depths by a vessel with a crane. The multitude stood with bared heads as Beachey's body was extricated and wrapped in a canvas shroud to be carried ashore.

The early exhibition fliers—of whom Lincoln Beachey was the ultimate example—believed that anything was possible in the air and that risk was the price of progress. More than that, they found in flying an exhilarating sense of freedom and a heady feeling of uniqueness (often accompanied by adulation and applause) that were heightened, not

Banking his Curtiss Special around a racetrack turn at Columbus, Ohio, in 1914, Lincoln Beachey ("The Daredevil of the Air") pulls ahead of Barney Oldfield ("The Demon of the Ground"), in a Fiat. The rivalry proved so popular that Beachey and Oldfield raced in 30 cities that summer.

diminished, by the awful risks they ran. Their public, violent and increasingly frequent deaths created for their kind a romantic legend.

But when Beachey died in 1915, such spectacles were being replaced by a more compelling and far more tragic drama—World War I. The fame of the early touring aviators was eclipsed as both sides explored the military uses of flying machines, by new legends of the Red Baron, Billy Bishop, Eddie Rickenbacker and the Lafayette Escadrille.

The tactical importance of aircraft was evident by the time the United States entered the War in 1917 and the hard-pressed British and French sought more planes and pilots from their new ally. Congress appropriated $640 million, and the vast productive machinery of the country began turning out thousands of training planes in which thousands of young men were hastily introduced to the narcotic delights of flying. But the War ended before most of these men could reach the front.

The 767 surviving American combat pilots and some 9,000 novice fliers faced a return to humdrum lives beneath peaceful skies. The

San Francisco

AN AMERICAN PAPER

Monarch of

VOL. CII.   MONDAY   SAN FRANCISCO, MARCH

BEACHEY IS KILLED DOING

Plunges 2,500 Feet to B.

The two-line banner in a San Francisco newspaper screams the news of Lincoln Beachey's fatal crash while he was performing his most dangerous stunt before some 50,000 onlookers in 1915.

throbbing new aircraft industry found itself producing multitudes of machines that suddenly had no useful purpose. The aviators, and aviation itself, seemed out of place in a world made safe for democracy.

It was then, in the quiet interlude after the clamor of war, that the spiritual legacy of Lincoln Beachey and the early exhibition fliers—their kind of philosophical recklessness—suddenly took on new relevance. Young men who had been abruptly denied the excitement of flight were dismayed at the prospect of going back to classrooms or drugstore counters. The United States was awash with cheap airplanes. The result was inevitable—a locust-like invasion of the American countryside by dashing young fliers, and a new direction for aviation.

These freewheeling barnstormers and speed kings and the self-appointed aircraft designers of the 1920s and 1930s were deplored by editorial writers, by government agencies and by manufacturers grown big enough to hope for an orderly and profitable aviation establishment. But it is hard to imagine that any public relations firm could have conceived a phenomenon better calculated to sell the airplane to the American public. Air shows and air races created headline after headline and made the names of fliers like Frank Hawks, Roscoe Turner and Jimmy Doolittle almost as familiar to newspaper readers as Babe Ruth, Jack Dempsey and Red Grange. Barnstorming pilots not only brought aviation to 10,000 rural pastures but were greeted as begoggled figures of romance when they climbed out of their open cockpits wearing shiny riding boots and white silk scarves. They lured vast numbers of their fellow citizens into the air: One group, the Gates Flying Circus, reportedly carried 750,000 joy-riding passengers aloft without a serious accident before disbanding in the face of government regulation in 1928.

The individual barnstormers, the salaried pilots of the aerial circuses

and their wingwalkers and stunt men were all creatures, in one way or another, of the fabled Curtiss Jenny—a plane available in such numbers after World War I that no American who itched to fly was denied that means of risking his neck.

This historic biplane had its beginnings in February 1914, when a United States Army board banned pusher planes because their engines—mounted just behind the pilot's perch—had been crushing fliers regularly after breaking loose during crash landings. Glenn Curtiss responded with his Model N—a plane with the engine mounted in front. During a visit to the Sopwith Aviation Company in England, he met an engineer named B. Douglas Thomas and talked him into designing an improved biplane designated Model J. It was decided to blend the best features of both craft into one, and Curtiss, at his Hammondsport, New York, factory, was soon producing JN-1s and evolving variations designated JN-2, JN-3 and so on until the JN-4D became the standard model. All were quickly embraced by the nickname Jenny.

Production reached 100 per month after the company built a new factory in Buffalo, New York. With entry of the United States into the War, commissioned subcontractors in eight other American cities began to build Jennies too. The Canadians, meanwhile, turned out a slightly altered, more maneuverable version called the Canuck.

By Armistice Day, some 6,000 Jennies had been produced for the United States government (at $5,000 per plane) and 2,000 more for governments abroad. The flow did not stop then. More than 2,000 additional Jennies were turned out before Washington got around to turning off the faucet for good. Thousands of these planes became surplus goods when the War was over, and even they did not constitute the whole market in cheap, eminently flyable aircraft.

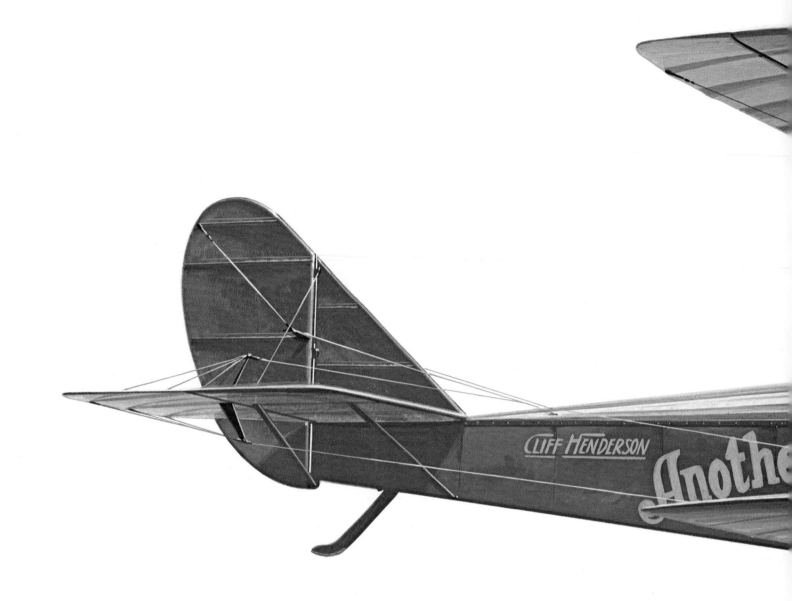

The ubiquitous Jenny

The fabled Curtiss JN-4D "Jenny," America's principal civilian aircraft of the early 1920s, was more a product of systematic trial and error than of inspired design. Keeping its temperamental OX-5 engine adequately cool, for example, required cutting away much of its leather-strapped cowling. Its short exhaust pipes spat fumes and oil in the pilot's face and on some occasions even ignited the explosive nitrate dope on the plane's fabric covering.

The Jenny's thin wings were braced by wooden struts and meticulously rigged with a maze of turnbuckled wires. As in many aircraft of the day, semicircular wing skids were added after wobbly landings on the narrow landing gear frequently ended with one wing dug into the ground. For all its flaws, the Jenny was an important evolutionary step in aircraft design, even though it was sometimes described as "a bunch of parts flying in formation."

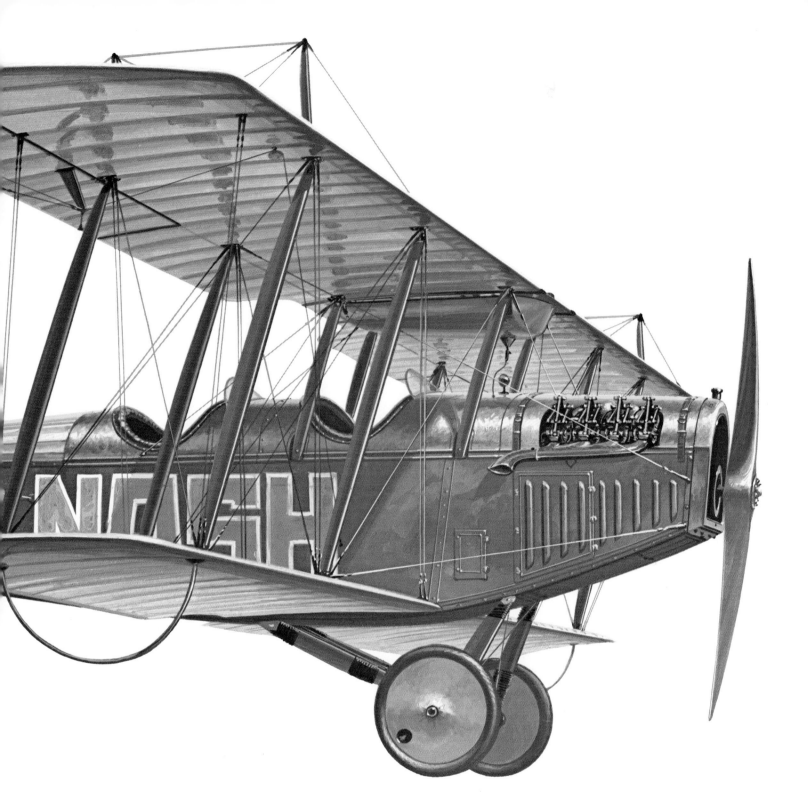

CURTISS JN-4D (JENNY)
One of some 10,000 JN-4Ds produced during and just after World War I, this Jenny belonged to Clifford Henderson, who used it, before he became the promoter of the National Air Races, as a flying advertisement for his Nash automobile agency in California.

The Standard Aircraft Company of Plainfield, New Jersey, had developed a two-place trainer similar to the Jenny—but, in fact, its aerodynamic superior—only to have it phased out during the War when its Hall-Scott engine developed a nasty habit of catching fire in mid-air. A thousand or more of these planes reposed, all brand-new, in storage facilities when hostilities ceased. Once reequipped with Hispano-Suiza engines, they became the most cherished of the aircraft in which the gypsy barnstormers plied their haphazard trade in the 1920s.

But Standards with Hissos were too costly for most fliers, who relied on the Jenny and its cruder Curtiss OX-5 engine, just as cowboys of an earlier generation had relied on the hardmouthed and recalcitrant bronco of the plains. The Jenny had comforting aspects. It could be landed at 45 miles per hour or, with modified high-lift wings, as slowly as 35. A pilot about to crash could aim his Jenny at a haystack or direct it between two trees—to dissipate energy as the wooden framework of the wings splintered and folded back—and could usually walk away.

Its limitations, however, were legion. Like all planes of the day it had no brakes, and anyone who landed it too fast risked hitting fences or ditches. It had a rated ceiling of 6,500 feet but seldom achieved it, as many a flier discovered while trying to surmount Appalachian passes at

A Pied Piper with wings, barnstormer Harold Watson draws a bevy of mesmerized youngsters in 1918 as he brings his Jenny to Morristown, New Jersey. It was the first plane to land there.

less than 4,000 feet. The landing wheels and tail skid were connected to the aircraft with an elastic binding known as bungee cord that barely diminished the aircraft's tendency to buck like a rodeo bronc if not returned to earth with precision. A barnstormer's plane spent its life out of doors in all weathers, and this constant exposure loosened its glue joints, rusted its flying wires and rotted its fabric.

The OX-5 engine, a water-cooled V-8 rated optimistically at 90 horsepower, was notoriously undependable. Its camshaft had a way of shattering in flight, and it was draped with external plumbing that leaked continuously and at times came loose, spewing hot water with disastrous results. Its standard magneto was less than reliable; wise pilots substituted a model known to the trade as the Scintilla, detached it when selling or abandoning a tired Jenny and guarded it jealously until reinstalling it on a fresh plane. And the flier who decided, while landing, to open his throttle, pull up and try again was taking a definite risk. The OX-5 had a way of coughing a few times before going back to work.

The gypsy flier became, of necessity, his own mechanic, rigger and, in a sense, designer—moved by the thin hope of modifying his plane to cure its more heinous failings. Scores of back-shop inventors and dealers in surplus equipment sprang up to assist him. He could buy newly covered secondhand wings for $30, reconditioned ailerons, rudders or elevators for $2.50 apiece and a newly overhauled OX-5 for $75. Advertisements in aviation magazines offered "toothpick propellers"— sharply tapered at each end—that were guaranteed to increase his engine's revolutions per minute no matter how weary it might have become. Thus, in time hundreds of Jennies achieved new individuality and, in many cases, new and unexpected patterns of behavior.

These restless ex-military pilots followed the sun as they barnstormed, traded five-minute rides for gasoline money or an occasional pint of moonshine whiskey, filched eggs from rural henhouses and boiled them in their breakfast coffee over campfires, and slept under the wings of their planes when darkness fell. They learned tricks of survival by necessity as they made their uncertain way, often without maps, over a countryside devoid of airports or weather forecasters.

The barnstorming gypsy learned to use cows as weather vanes, since they turned their tails to the wind, but to regard them with suspicion on the ground because they had an awful habit of licking the nitrate dope from the wings of untended aircraft, leaving the fabric surfaces sagging dolefully from their underlying spars. He contrived to doctor a misfiring engine or to patch a fuselage with spare fabric and pieces of packing crate—on pain of finding himself marooned, perhaps for good, in some meadow far from the nearest town.

He searched for rural garages as he flew and landed as near them as possible; they were his source of fuel and he had to carry his gasoline cans to his plane—sometimes for long distances. He strained the stuff through a chamois skin (hoping wistfully to keep water—which actually collected through condensation—out of his tank) and sometimes add-

A handbill circulated in Kankakee, Illinois, to drum up a crowd for Dale A. Seitz's barnstormers in 1926 emphasizes the team's "Safe and Sane" motto. They promised not to stunt with passengers on board.

ed moth balls in an attempt to increase the performance of his engine. He sealed leaky radiators—with varying success—by adding a handful of bran while pouring in water.

Meanwhile, since his living depended on it, the barnstormer hunted the back country for people willing to part with cash for a ride in his front cockpit. Basil Lee Rowe, a World War I mechanic-turned-peacetime flier, developed a typical system of testing a town for profitability as he barnstormed down the East Coast. "I would buzz it a couple of times," he said. "If the people continued about their business, I did the same. But if the animals and fowl took off for the woods and the kids tried to follow me, I looked for a farmer's field from which to operate. When I found one, I buzzed the town to get the whole population following me like the children of Hamelin following the Pied Piper."

But selling rides to residents of rural areas became increasingly difficult, as even the most isolated of farmers became accustomed to seeing the gypsy planes. Pilots compensated by banding together in twos and threes and putting on little air shows to draw crowds. They flew loops, hired volunteer parachute jumpers and took turns climbing out of their cockpits while compatriots flew their planes, clutching the struts and wires that festooned the wings of their battered biplanes. (It was said that if a bird could fly unscathed between the wings from front to back, a wire was missing.) They were indebted for many of their new techniques to a star-crossed man who immediately after the War succeeded Lincoln Beachey as the most celebrated aerial exhibitionist in the world.

Ormer Leslie Locklear led a life far different from those of the barnstormers he was to influence. He earned as much as $3,000 a day, lived in fancy hotels, performed for vast crowds in big cities and became an international celebrity and a darling of Hollywood. But he sprang from the same roots, was driven by the same need for self-dramatization, and suffered and rejected the same premonitions of disaster as other aerial daredevils. He was above all an innovator; his career lasted only 16 months, but he epitomized the attitudes of the pilots and stunt men of barnstorming troupes and motion pictures long after his death.

Locklear was a carpenter and mechanic in Fort Worth, Texas, when he enlisted in the Army Air Service, at the age of 26, on October 25, 1917. He became a celebrity within months of arriving at Texas' Barron Field by climbing out of the cockpit of a Jenny flown by a fellow officer and walking around on its lower wing among the struts and wires. Locklear soon contrived more hair-raising aerial acrobatics. He boosted himself from a Jenny's fuselage to its upper wing and stood erect and unsupported there, leaning into the wind to maintain a precarious balance. (As a dashing aviator, he stubbornly insisted, while performing this stunt, on wearing his riding boots with their slippery leather soles rather than tennis shoes.) He soon contrived a method of changing planes in mid-air—hanging by his hands from the landing gear of one Jenny and letting go to sprawl on the upper wing of another.

The slow landing speed of the Jenny saved Howard Casterline in 1928 from any personal damage beyond embarrassment and a bumped nose. Approaching a cornfield outside Hartford City, Indiana, at dusk, Casterline crashed into a tree. He gingerly climbed down and walked away.

Locklear and his two confederates—a big Alabaman named Milton "Skeets" Elliott and a former college student from Pennsylvania, James Frew—were risking court martial, among other things, as stunting was strictly forbidden. But the Army was killing too many flying cadets in trying to push them through its crowded training fields; Locklear's commanding officer hit on the idea of using him and his co-conspirators to restore the morale of student pilots by convincing them that Jennies were not necessarily instruments of certain death. The three fliers were henceforth encouraged to perform for their fellows.

Locklear stayed on in the service after the Armistice and refined his reckless gymnastics, thanks in good part to increasingly precise formation flying by Elliott and a new teammate, Lieutenant Shirley J. "Shorty" Short, whom they recruited when Frew decided to return to civilian life. Locklear contrived a frightening new stunt—hopping across empty space from one wing tip to another as the two pilots labored to keep their planes flying evenly, side by side.

He became the beneficiary, in the spring of 1919, of a chance meeting with William Hickman Pickens, a fast-talking entrepreneur and press agent who considered himself the world's greatest practitioner of the art of ballyhoo. Pickens had drummed up great audiences by sensationalizing the careers of Lincoln Beachey, racing driver Barney Oldfield and female parachutist Tiny Broadwick, but he sensed that Locklear might outdo all his previous clients at the box office. He wasted no time in making an offer of fame and fortune the flier could not resist.

Elliott and Short were soon persuaded, and all three resigned from the service to accept their Svengali's conditions of employment. Pickens demanded 50 per cent of all profits. He insisted that they perform "despite rain, shine and cyclone." But he was, he said, "willing to risk a generous dollar provided the other man would chance his neck," and he backed his word by spending $6,000 on three brand-new Jennies. He also planned the lavish use of illustrated advertising in courting the public. "If mishandled properly," he liked to say, "a good lithograph can make a school picnic look like the third day at Gettysburg."

To shield himself from embarrassment in the event his client turned out to be a flop, Pickens chose backwater Uniontown, Pennsylvania, as the site of Locklear's introductory performance. But after the pilot dazzled a crowd of 10,000, Pickens presented him to big-time reporters and the elite of the aviation establishment at the Second Annual Pan American Aeronautic Congress, in Atlantic City. Finding himself with one of the hottest properties in show business, Pickens contemplated what he later described as the "golden renaissance of barnstorming."

Promoters bombarded Pickens with requests for his new star's services. But the press agent warned Locklear that the public would soon tire of him unless he could contrive new, more sensational gimmicks. Locklear responded, at Erie, Pennsylvania, with a stunt he had never rehearsed: grabbing the ladder under Elliott's plane while standing in an automobile being driven around a track at the exhibition grounds.

He was yanked over the automobile's windshield and dragged along the track. The aircraft was unable to rise. Locklear let go and went tumbling spectacularly along the ground. But he got groggily to his feet with no injury more serious than cuts on his hands and face, and he was in Chicago performing again just two days later. Locklear fretted over the bandages he was forced to wear—he told Pickens that they might suggest that flying was not safe and, worse yet, might cause customers to shun his performances. "Bandages are box office," cried Pickens, who had set his client's minimum price at $1,000. "Don't ever forget that we're both capitalizing on sudden death!"

But Pickens was afraid, with good reason, that imitators would kill the goose that was laying his golden eggs. Frank Clarke, a barnstormer working near Hollywood, heard of Locklear's plane change and decided to try it. As the second plane came close enough for him to grab its wing skid, it hit turbulence and its wing tip smashed into Clarke's jaw, knocking him down on the wing of his craft. Recovering, he tried again, missed the skid, and almost toppled into space. He made it on the third try—thus launching a brilliant career as a movie stunt man.

Pickens had decided to sell Locklear to the movies while the selling was good. "For a huge sum," announced the Universal Film Company, "Lieutenant Locklear has agreed to appear in the leading role of a big six reel feature . . . in which will be interpolated all of his amazing feats of acrobatics." Locklear was euphoric from the moment of his arrival at Los Angeles in midsummer of 1919. Hollywood was mad about aviation, and Locklear, accepted instantly as the kingpin of American fliers, found himself rubbing shoulders with admiring heroes and heroines of the silent screen. He responded by diving on motion-picture lots, running his wheels over the curved roofs of their big indoor stages—a stunt that became known as the "Locklear Bounce"—and by doing a little wingwalking for the edification of studio people.

He found life in Hollywood more captivating yet after he met Viola Dana, a dark-haired beauty who had moved upward from Brooklyn, New York (where she had been Viola Flugrath), to leading roles and a salary of $2,250 a week at the Metro studios. Locklear, though he had a wife at home in Texas, was entranced. Viola was entranced too, and, in contrast to Locklear's wife, she reacted to his recklessness with unconcealed fascination. She was flattered when he landed his Jenny on Cahuenga Boulevard to pick her up after work and when he set down on the beach to join her for a dip. They soon were inseparable.

In Universal's *Great Air Robbery* Locklear was called upon to scramble up a rope ladder from one plane to another to save a drunken fellow pilot, repeat the stunt to rescue the heroine, then hang from the landing gear of a plane, drop into a speeding automobile, beat up a crook, grab the heroine's jewels and get back into the plane by way of the landing gear as the car went spectacularly out of control.

It was a heady experience. Locklear was soon to be outdone by other motion-picture stunt pilots—among them Dick Grace, Frank Clarke,

Ormer Locklear flashes the confident grin that matched his reputation as a fearless aviator. He performed such stunts as the "Dance of Death" (right), in which he and another pilot flew with their wing tips overlapping—then exchanged places. The Los Angeles airfield below them was owned by Charlie Chaplin's brother, Sydney.

Paul Mantz and Al Wilson—but he set new standards of daring in *The Great Air Robbery* and basked in the admiration of the film colony as a result. But not for long. Pickens soon wrenched him away from Viola and rushed him forth, with Elliott, Short and two mechanics, to perform at 22 air shows and fairs in 15 states from August to November of 1919. More and more imitators were copying his stunts—by autumn eight of them had killed themselves in the process—but Locklear felt he had reached the apogee of his career during this tour; the onetime carpenter from Texas was being heralded as the king of the barnstormers.

The constant strain of stunting, however, left him subject to a gnawing awareness of his own mortality and a growing preoccupation with death. During a mid-air transfer at the Illinois State Fair he had almost

toppled from the wing when the iron bar weighting the rope ladder hit him on the forehead, opening a nasty gash. He had hoped for a rest after the Midwest tour, but Pickens insisted on his performing at a series of air shows in California, and the bar hit him again, knocking him sprawling, as he desperately tried to seize the ladder in a high wind over San Francisco. He pulled himself up to Elliott's Jenny on the 11th attempt, but admitted, while wiping blood from his face after landing, that he had endured "the hardest day of flying I have ever done."

He held on to a comforting prospect: that he would soon, thanks to his growing fame, be able to quit barnstorming and devote himself solely to acting. And when, in April 1920, the William Fox Studios offered him $1,650 a week to appear in a new thriller, *The Skywayman*, he was exhilarated at the prospect of resuming his career as an actor. But Pickens minced no words in reminding him of his contractual obligations and in outlining his future: Locklear, Short and Elliott were to tour the Midwest and South as soon as the picture was finished, producing the "supreme sensation" Pickens had been promising the public.

Locklear reacted perversely when told that the studio had hit on a way of eliminating risk from a dramatic night scene in which he was to spin toward earth from 2,000 feet. Fox camera experts would simulate darkness by using panchromatic film and filters while shooting in broad daylight. Locklear wanted no part of such faking; his audience would be given the real thing. Astonished Fox executives finally gave in, but to protect their investment in case the star was killed they insisted on finishing the rest of the picture before doing the controversial scene.

As he prepared for his big scene, on August 2, 1920, Locklear seemed invigorated. The Jenny he was to fly had been painted white to make it more visible against the night sky. Five 100,000-candle-power arc lights had been positioned, aimed skyward, in a semicircle around the field to cast a pool of peripheral illumination in which his plane could be seen, and to provide him with vertical references before he ignited magnesium flares on his wings to simulate a flaming crash.

Locklear asked Viola, as he led her through a rapidly growing crowd on the evening of the shooting, if she would like to squeeze into the front cockpit with Skeets Elliott and come along. She was delighted and argued heatedly with him when he suddenly changed his mind, muttering, "I've a hunch I ought not to fly tonight." She stayed on the ground.

The plane vanished into the darkness, appearing moments later at 3,000 feet, mothlike in the illumination of the arc lights. Locklear looped and rolled for 15 minutes and then, igniting the flares on his wing tips— prompting a sudden, admiring outcry from the crowd—dived like a great, descending Roman candle to 2,000 feet, pulled up in a stall and began spinning, counterclockwise, toward the ground. His audience watched in fascinated silence. But as he reached 500 feet, they began to scream, "Cut the lights! Cut the lights!" which appeared to be blinding him. Instead, the arcs began swinging toward the plane and, one by one, trapped it in their shafts of light.

Inviting movie-goers to "watch the sky" for them on opening night, local fliers hired by the Rivoli Theatre parade their flying boat—its wings removed for transport—through Portland, Oregon, in 1920. They were part of the national publicity campaign promoting Ormer Locklear's first film, The Great Air Robbery.

The brilliantly illuminated white Jenny went into a vertical dive at 300 feet and plummeted to earth near an oil derrick that stood beyond the field. The sound of its engine ceased. An explosion followed. A pool of sludge caught fire and cast a bright yellow glare into the night.

Few Americans ever went to their graves amid such clamor as did Ormer Locklear. His death prompted headlines from coast to coast. His casket was escorted to the Los Angeles railroad station, with Elliott's, by a police band, a military honor guard, a troupe of movie cowboys and a long line of automobiles (including a chauffered limousine in which Viola rode alone) while a squadron of airplanes circled overhead.

Fifty thousand people lined the streets of Fort Worth, where he was to be buried, to watch his funeral cortege. Twenty thousand more gathered around the church where the services were held, and 15,000 came to the cemetery where he was laid to rest. Pickens did not attend.

Many publications responded to the whole episode with disapproval.

"We do not," the London *Evening News* noted stiffly, "want this kind of thing in England." The *Los Angeles Herald,* however, saluted "such serene composure in the face of danger . . . as shames mere pygmy mortals who shiver, quake and are afraid." But it was *The Los Angeles Times* that spoke most realistically: It was shocked at the tragic death of "such fine young men," but admitted that "their loss is not likely to deter other audacious young fliers."

Between 500 and 600 undeterred and audacious young fliers barnstormed the country, according to an estimate by the Aeronautical Chamber of Commerce, in the years following Locklear's spectacular death. Their lives were less ornate than Locklear's had been (one said the chief peril of the occupation was starvation) but fully as romantic.

The difficulties, discomforts and genuine perils of the gypsy pilot's lot were visited typically and in full measure on R. C. "Tex" Marshall and his friend Frank Palmer after they left Sea Breeze, Florida, for Findlay, Ohio, in May 1920. They were grounded in Augusta, Georgia, by a typical barnstormer condition—lack of cash. Marshall rode into South Carolina by train and found 4,000 people—the entire populace of a town named Edgefield—who not only had never seen an airplane but were willing to build a landing field in order to do so. Marshall had doubts about the only cleared ground available, as he wrote later. "This plot was 1,000 feet long and 150-200 feet wide, but it had gullies in it four feet deep and ridges five and six feet high and rocks and big stumps on three sides surrounded by high trees." But he stifled his misgivings.

"We had about 40 men, tractors and dynamite galore and after four and a half days of the hardest work I ever did the field was fairly smooth. I was afraid that it was so soft that we would be unable to take off, and would probably be hung to boot, for those people sure were crazy to see the planes. I got Frank on the phone and told him to hop right over. He landed right and we gave the mayor a ride and he was the happiest man I had seen in a long time. I got on the train and hurtled over to Augusta after my plane." The passengers were lined up the next morning when he returned, and the pilots had so much business that afternoon "it seemed that time, like us, flew on wings." Marshall and Palmer were richer by $500 when they flew away three days later and were able to pay their way during the long month it took them to reach Ohio.

Such gypsies were not above crossing into Canada and Mexico in pursuit of adventure and cash. Those in the Southwest had opportunities to make real money, thanks to Prohibition and import taxes, by flying contraband across the Mexican border. Few of them entered into smuggling with the enthusiasm of Floyd Hurtial "Slats" Rodgers, a diminutive ex-railroad engineer from Texas. Rodgers had built his own airplane in 1912—a contraption he called "Old Soggy No. 1." He learned through trial and error that he could get it into the air only by bouncing it off a knoll at full speed and that he could keep its wings level only by leaning constantly to his left while seated at the controls. This unnerving process, which he equated with "driving a blind hog to water," left him immune to the comparatively minor eccentricities of the Jennies and Standards he flew in the 1920s—or the dangers of smuggling, into which he entered wholeheartedly after finding that he could make $8,000 by flying a load of whiskey across the border from Mexico.

Well known to lawmen and smugglers for his contraband operations, Rodgers was better known to the public as the ringleader, at Dallas, Texas, of the self-styled "Lunatics of Love Field," a band of barnstormers dedicated, Rodgers said, to "seeing which one could come closest to getting the motor in his eye without really getting it there."

"I might have stayed with flying, I mean hauling passengers, if it had stayed the way it was," he later recalled. "But here came the Gypsy Barnstormers from other parts of the country, horning in. People would pay to go up once, maybe two or three times. Then they wouldn't pay any more. Before long you ran out of customers."

Before long the fliers found, out of desperate necessity, that stunting could bring the customers back. "I figured what the crowd loved was noise and low flying," reasoned Rodgers, and he quickly learned to swoop down in front of his audience, touch the ground with his wheels and go into a loop from an altitude of zero. "It worked," he said, "even if I did get gravel in my face sometimes from my own prop wash."

Wingwalking became a standard part of the barnstormers' repertoire, and one Gene Brewer practiced the risky art as a member of the Love Field Lunatics. Brewer began climbing a seven-foot ladder atop the upper wing of Rodgers' plane on one occasion—as Slats prepared to execute a loop over a state fair in Dallas—but fell off in the process and tumbled into the cockpit on top of the pilot. One of his pants legs slipped over the control stick. "There I was," said Rodgers, "my flying controls up Gene Brewer's pants leg. There's no use asking me why things like that happened to me. They did. I told him to hold on and I'd try to land the ship by holding on to his leg and the stick, too." They made it.

But as the years passed pilots found their Jennies aging, the crowds growing jaded, and the law of averages working against them. Rodgers bought a supposedly reconditioned Jenny for a 1923 air show in Wichita Falls and asked a mechanic to pull the prop through a couple of times to load the cylinders with gas for easier starting as he prepared to take off from Love Field. "The switch is off," he yelled, and it was indeed in the "off" position, but the engine started for all that. The startled mechanic escaped injury and Rodgers took blithely to the air. He had mounted a siren on the undercarriage to attract attention to the air show. He turned it on, listened to its satisfying howl, and tried to turn it off. The cutoff would not work. He then noticed that the engine was running too fast, and pulled back on the throttle. It broke. The engine began to run faster and faster. "There I was," he said, "Siren wide open, throttle wide open, engine roaring to beat hell, about to fly apart any minute, and I couldn't cut off anything."

He circled the field at Wichita Falls for an hour and 10 minutes—

Locklear and copilot Milton Elliott smash through a breakaway steeple, rousting a pair of stunt-man villains in a scene from The Skywayman.

since he was flying too fast to land—and ran out of gas, before heading, finally, for the ground. But more gas ran into the carburetor as the tail dropped, the engine fired up at full speed and he was back in the air. He ran out of gas once more and landed. He jumped out and grabbed a wing tip when the plane touched down—just as yet more gas entered the carburetor. "Round and round we went, me digging up dirt with my heels, the motor roaring. The men around the field were afraid to come out. They didn't know which way the ship was going next. When they finally did get to the ship I was all out of breath, but I was still hanging on and the motor was just sputtering." Asked what the matter was, Rodgers growled, "You think of something that ain't the matter."

The consequences were not always so benign. In 1923 barnstormers were involved in 179 accidents in which 85 people were killed and 126 injured. There was growing opposition to the carnage, both within aviation circles and without. Editorials calling for restrictions were especially strident when spectators or passengers died, as they often did. Many pilots and aircraft builders believed that barnstorming was giving aviation a bad name by drawing attention to its risks instead of emphasizing the safety, increasing reliability and usefulness of aircraft.

By the middle of the decade the first wave of barnstormers, the military-trained fliers, had been well thinned out. The capable pilots had become fixed-base operators or had regular jobs testing aircraft or flying the mail. The bad or unlucky ones had been killed, and the indifferent ones had drifted out of the game. Barnstormers by 1925 were largely younger men whose zeal for flying had been ignited by the postwar gypsy fliers. Haphazardly trained, unseasoned by experience and uneducated in the capabilities of their aircraft or the basics of flight, many were a real threat to the lives of their trusting passengers (it was not unknown for a pilot to make his first solo flight in the morning and haul passengers for hire in the afternoon) and the spectators who watched.

It became more difficult to attract passengers, and the price of a ride dropped from $15 to as low as one dollar. It became harder and harder to keep the airplanes in the air, for while income was dropping, the cost of repairing the aging crates was going up. Struggling aviators thus had many reasons to band together in flying circuses or to join established circuses—which offered regular pay, professional advertising and management and the proper maintenance of adequate aircraft. The day of the gypsy flier ended for good after the United States Congress enacted the Air Commerce Act of 1926. The Lunatics were apprised of their own demise by way of a government bulletin tacked up at Love Field. The Aeronautics Branch of the Department of Commerce warned them that it would henceforth license pilots and mechanics, would register and certify aircraft and would regulate air traffic. Licenses for pilots and registration numbers for aircraft were to be issued by a department inspector, and compliance would be required by July 1927. "I didn't know at first what the bulletin meant," said Slats Rodgers. "Actually, it meant that my way of flying and living was coming to an end." ～

Captain Percival Phillips buzzes a popular resort beach in Kent in order to attract paying passengers in 1928.

Barnstorming in Britain

After World War I, Britain had its share of proven pilots and planes—and the public had a yen to experience the novelty of flying. In 1924, Captain Percival Phillips, formerly of the Royal Flying Corps, launched the Cornwall Aviation Company with a single reconditioned Avro biplane that he had bought for £250.

Touring seaside resorts and inland pastures, Phillips offered five-minute rides for five shillings and expanded into a flying circus that offered a repertoire of aerial thrills and laughs. At the height of their popularity, Phillips' planes were taking up 500 passengers a day, and by the time the Cornwall Aviation Company ceased operations in 1937, he and other British barnstormers had lured more than a million of their countrymen into the air.

Already looking somewhat airsick, the apprehensive mayor (right) and town clerk of Woolwich prepare for a turn at joy riding in 1928 by crowding into the rear cockpit of Captain Phillips' Avro.

The field announcer (left) and costumed crew of Phillips' flying circus strike a theatrical pose at a Somerset airfield in 1931 after parading through town to drum up a crowd for that day's show.

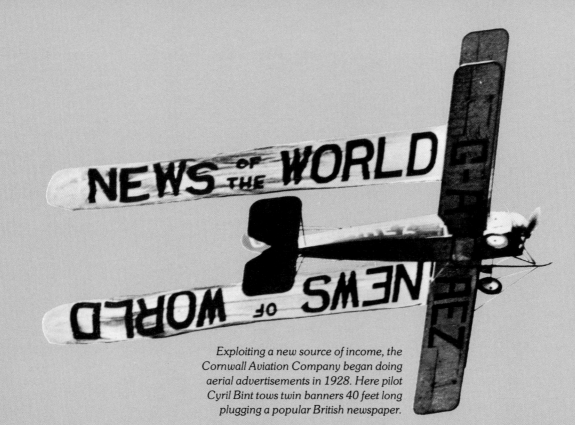

Exploiting a new source of income, the Cornwall Aviation Company began doing aerial advertisements in 1928. Here pilot Cyril Bint tows twin banners 40 feet long plugging a popular British newspaper.

In this view from another aircraft, a circus plane dives on a crowd at Plymouth in 1932, with wingwalker Martin Hearn holding on by a wire.

2
Hectic heyday
of the flying circus

Joseph R. James was enjoying his life as a commercial pilot in the summer of 1927, but he left his old Curtiss Oriole tied to a fence at Elmhurst, Illinois, and "packed furiously" on receiving a telegram from Major Ivan Gates: JOIN US AT TETERBORO FIELD. FIFTY DOLLARS A WEEK AND EXPENSES GUARANTEED. It was, he said later, "the ultimate achievement for any barnstormer in the country"—a job offer from the Gates Flying Circus.

The touring Gates organization was by 1927 drawing as many as 30,000 spectators to each of its performances, was selling rides to 100,000 passengers a year and had established itself as "The Daddy of the Air Circuses." James was summoned to the circus's newly acquired permanent headquarters near Teterboro Airport in New Jersey, where Fokker aircraft and Wright Whirlwind engines were manufactured. An abandoned wooden factory building—on which was emblazoned the legend: GATES FLYING CIRCUS, GREATEST AVIATORS IN THE WORLD, and which looked to James like a "great old red barn"—housed a shop devoted to overhauling engines and refurbishing the circus's aging five-place Standards.

Fliers drifted in and out of Gates's employ, and by 1927 there were 11 "shabby but always arrogant young eagles," as James described them, ready to take to the air. Few pilots, no matter what their backgrounds, wasted any time in heading for Teterboro if they were invited to join the illustrious ranks of the Gates troupe. James was no exception, but he learned at once that life with the flying circus was not always as glamorous as he had assumed. He was led into the old factory building on arrival, handed a pair of overalls and told one of the outfit's few rules: Pilots were personally responsible for the condition of their planes. "I walked over to my ship, an uncovered skeleton of a J-1 Standard fuselage," he recalled, "and spent the rest of the day assembling and inspecting it."

Also on that first day, James was introduced to Ivan Gates himself, whom he described as "a man in his early forties, blond, grizzled, about five feet seven inches and powerfully built." He was, said James, "high potentate and general manager of the circus, known by his daredevils as 'The Pope.'"

Gates, a Californian born in Rockford, Michigan, was a hot-tempered individualist who often expressed himself with his fists when confronted by those incautious enough to oppose or ignore him. Nor did he limit

Sipping a drink through a straw while hanging upside down, Myrtle "Mimsi" Mims rehearses for an assault on the endurance record for inverted flight, while her partner-husband, Luke, reads a newspaper. Like other circus fliers, the Mimses found that they needed to try strange and risky stunts to catch the increasingly fickle eye of the crowds on the air-show circuit.

47

his violence to people. Once, trying to get in touch with an advance man in Gainesville, Florida, he sent a telegram addressed, TRY HOTELS, a standard instruction meaning that the operator should call hotels until the man was found. When he was informed later that the message had not gone through because there was no "Try" hotel in Gainesville, he tore his phone off the wall, jumped on it and swore never again to use Western Union.

Pilots took an astonishingly benign view of Gates's habit of swinging for the jaw when he was aroused, in part because he nursed no grudges, in part because he was invariably abashed after flooring some unfortunate and often stuffed a few greenbacks into the victim's handiest pocket on helping him to his feet. He liked to tell reporters that he had flown pusher planes before World War I and that he had once carried a reluctant convict—supposedly the first prisoner ever to be transferred by air—from San Bernardino to San Francisco. The fact is that he did not learn to fly at all until the flying circus was already well established and his own reputation as a promoter was no longer in need of such false publicity.

Gates made flying the province of Clyde Edward "Upside Down" Pangborn, chief pilot and half owner of the circus. Joe James was not only impressed but subtly chastened, as were most fliers, on meeting Pangborn for the first time. "I shall never forget his steady penetrating gray eyes and his serious mien. At that time he was about 30 years old, lean, wiry and blond. He was never known to drink or smoke and reputedly had more flying hours to his credit than any other single man in the game. He had very little to say but I knew this expert pilot would watch my every move."

Pangborn was an engineer from St. Maries, Idaho, who had learned to fly in the Army, had served as an instructor in Texas and had begun barnstorming along the Pacific Coast in a surplus Jenny after the Armistice. As an Army flier he had spent his off-duty time in Texas diving on Houston streetcars and seeing how close he could come to knocking the gilded knobs off flagpoles—escaping retribution, it was said, by painting fake numbers on his trainer.

He specialized in flying upside down. This was a trick that demanded perfect timing and the ability to maintain a precise angle of glide, since a Jenny's engine was fed its fuel by gravity and would barely idle when it was inverted. Difficult or not, the stunt attracted few spectators to the San Diego field at which Pangborn was attempting, with another pilot named Ralph Reed, to make a living selling airplane rides. The spectators trooped out to watch, however, when Pangborn began climbing around the Jenny's fuselage and hanging by his feet from its landing gear. And he drew an enormous crowd to Coronado Beach when he promised to climb on board the aircraft, by way of a rope ladder, from a speeding automobile.

He all but killed himself as well. The automobile was going too slowly and the aircraft was too far to the left at the moment of contact, and

A handbill, one of thousands scattered from the air over America in the 1920s, promises a skyful of aerial action for a quarter when the daredevils of the Gates Flying Circus arrive in town.

Pangborn was hurled to the ground—as Ormer Locklear had been in trying the same trick—at 60 miles per hour. Pangborn severely injured the muscles of his shoulders and hips, dislocated three vertebrae, stretched his left wrist and split a bone in one elbow as he rolled and bounced along the hard sand. He sprang to his feet and bowed to the spectators, but he was crippled for weeks and fell prey to pneumonia that autumn after finally getting back into the air. He was living from hand to mouth, after two years of rising and falling fortune, when Ivan Gates hired him in 1922.

The promoter, who was determined to become the P. T. Barnum of aviation, soon acquired a wingwalker and some additional pilots and booked the Gates Flying Circus into city after city. He contracted with The Texas Company to receive free fuel and lubricants in return for painting his planes bright red with the legend TEXACO emblazoned across the lower wings and the company's trademark prominently displayed on each fuselage.

By 1924 the organization included three stunt men and three pilots: Pangborn (now a full partner in the enterprise), a specialist in dead-stick landings named A. R. "Tommy" Thompson and a loud-talking ex-Army flier, William C. "Whispering Bill" Brooks. They contrived, under Pangborn's leadership, a series of thrilling spectacles for their craning spectators. Pangborn, besides looping repeatedly in tight formation with his two colleagues, flew upside down within yards of the ground. Thompson climbed to 3,000 feet, cut his switch and did loops and wing overs with a dead engine. The stunt men changed planes and walked wings, and the pilots, after darkness fell, performed their aerial acrobatics with giant sparklers blazing on the wing tips of the planes. But the pilots kept the circus profitable primarily by carrying load after load of passengers aloft.

Pangborn's influence as a partner was not limited to his skill and leadership in the air. Gates was shrewd enough to realize that he needed Pangborn not only as a working aviator but as a foil for his own headstrong personality. The calm, laconic Pangborn soothed ruffled tempers, commanded the respect of other pilots and attracted a number of talented fliers, over the years, who made the Gates Flying Circus a squadron of the aerial elite.

Not that Gates and his fliers held a monopoly on organized barnstorming; they shared the skies and the farm fields of America with dozens of other aerial circuses. Most of these rickety enterprises worked their way around the country from pasture to pasture, small town to small town, as had the postwar gypsies who had banded together to form them—tacking up posters on barns and telephone poles after advertising their arrival by buzzing rooftops along Main Street with a stunt man out on one wing.

Such little outfits had some of the same difficulties with crowds as did their predecessors, the solo barnstormers. Farmers had a way of gathering across the road to watch the show without paying admission.

The circuses learned that morbid curiosity could lure many reluctant bystanders past the ticket sellers and they sometimes hired a local ambulance to drive into their pasture with its siren screaming. Another ruse was to send a plane aloft with a dummy in the front cockpit and allow it to fall to earth during a loop. This last stunt had a way of backfiring, however, for an amiable crowd could become an angry mob when it discovered that it had been tricked. The dummy was more commonly dropped before the show with advertising placards attached to its chest for the benefit of those who panted through the brush to find the "body."

Big or small, circuses did their best to offer at least one stunt unusual enough to extract cash from the most reluctant bystander. Eddie Angel of Jimmy Angel's Flying Circus specialized in a "Dive of Death"— jumping out of a plane after dark with a flashlight in each hand and opening his chute only when he could see the ground. Walter Hunter of Oklahoma's Hunter Brothers Flying Circus hung by his knees from the undercarriage of a plane and dropped into a haystack without any chute at all. Cliff Rose of the Cliff Rose Death Angels fastened "batman" wings to his arms and did spirals and other stunts before reaching for his rip cord. Roy Ahearn of the Tidewater Air Circus once bought an ancient Jenny for $300, tied sacks of gunpowder to its struts, slopped 10 gallons of oil and 25 gallons of gasoline on its wings and set it afire in the

Mabel Cody successfully transfers from a speeding boat to a rope ladder dangling from a Standard off St. Augustine, Florida, in 1926. She was the first woman to perform this stunt, and she had survived a previous attempt during which the plane crashed and the boat caught fire.

night sky over Cocoa Beach, Florida. He escaped with a parachute he had folded up and stuffed in the cockpit behind him before takeoff (but he did not make good his exit before expending some harrowing moments disentangling the cords from the knobs and levers of the cockpit of the burning ship).

Most of the flying circuses tried to avoid areas that had been recently visited by competitors and searched instead for pools of citizenry yet to be introduced to the performances of wingwalkers and parachute jumpers. A headstrong stunt woman named Mabel Cody, who had organized an exhibition team of her own, and the Doug Davis Flying Circus, which was drawing big audiences in Georgia and Alabama, flouted this practice in 1925 and made the South a kind of aerial battleground as they did so.

Douglas Davis was a walking testimonial to the value of persistence. Army instructors had despaired of ever teaching him to fly after he left his home in Griffin, Georgia, to join the Air Service during World War I. They seem to have agreed to his being commissioned only out of reluctant admiration for his willingness to risk killing himself as he staggered around the skies over Kelly Field near San Antonio, Texas. He refused to be discouraged, bought a used Jenny with his last dime after the Armistice and made a living with it by offering Georgia farmers two rides for the price of one.

Davis was quick to understand that a barnstormer had to entertain if he was to succeed. He hired other pilots, plus a stunt man who had been a circus trapeze artist, invaded the countryside in force and spent his profits on advertising, maintenance and new equipment. The Doug Davis circus certified its place in the hearts of rural Southerners and its dominance of Southern skies by grossing $1,400 during a single performance at Opelika, Alabama, during the summer of 1924. But Mabel Cody changed all that the following year.

A niece of the Wild West showman Buffalo Bill Cody, Mabel was nerveless, a remarkable acrobat and the star of her own circus. She made her name a byword by performing delayed parachute jumps, dancing on wings and, on one occasion, grabbing a rope ladder under one of her Jennies while tearing across a lake in a speedboat. She understood the value of ballyhoo and made the most of a loud-mouthed barker named Curly Burns, who urged spectators into the air by giving Mabel's pilots military rank that most of them did not possess. "The suckers," he liked to say, "go for that officer stuff."

Doug Davis recognized Mabel Cody as a formidable rival and proposed that she merge her show with his. "What's the matter, Doug?" she taunted, "Are you scared of a little girl like me?" But she spoke too soon. Davis began scheduling exhibitions near those at which Cody was to perform, plastering nearby barns with gaudy advertising posters, cutting his prices and opening his show two hours before hers. The customers, however, remained fascinated with Mabel—who was, after all, a woman. He did his best to lure her pilots away to work for him with

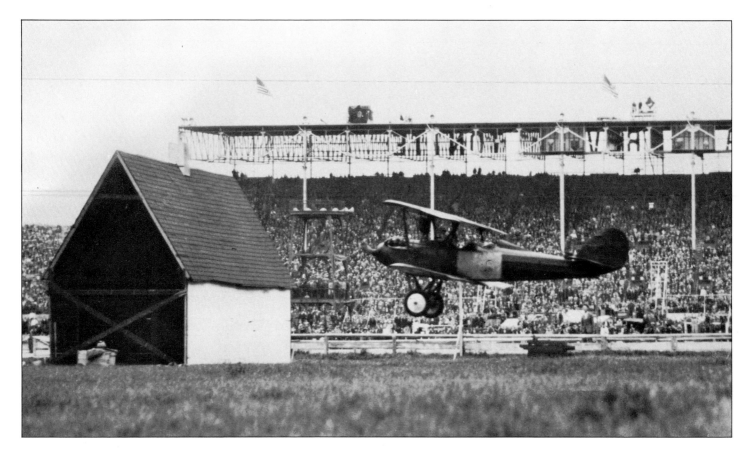

Frank "Bowser" Frakes's specialty was crashing into buildings, as he does in this sequence taken at the 1935 Minnesota State Fair. Two years later a version of the same stunt almost killed him when a fuel-soaked hut designed to ignite on impact collapsed, temporarily trapping him inside.

promises of higher wages, but they turned him down. And she fought back, bringing the Mabel Cody Flying Circus into towns Davis had scheduled one day ahead of him, thus emptying the townspeople's pockets before he arrived.

Davis prevailed because his planes remained airworthy, thanks to his constant, careful maintenance, while those of Mabel Cody's circus were increasingly grounded by deteriorating airframes and faulty engines. She joined forces with him in the end, and they toured together as costars of an air show promoting the greater glory of a candy bar: The Doug Davis Baby Ruth Flying Circus.

But if flying circuses tended to work the same territory, year after year, individual pilots and stunt men moved from circus to circus, and many of those based near Los Angeles barnstormed only as a way of staying busy between assignments from motion-picture studios. One collection of especially talented stunt fliers organized themselves as the 13 Black Cats in 1925. During the not-quite four years they stuck together they broke new ground by demanding set prices for a long list of stunts. The figures are illuminating. Among them:

> Crash ships (fly into trees, houses, etc.) $1,200
> Loop with man on each wing standing up $450
> Ship change $100
> Upside-down change $500
> Change—motorcycle to airplane $150
> Fight on upper wing, one man knocked off $225
> Upside-down flying with man on landing gear $150
> Head-on collision with automobiles $250
> Blow up plane in mid-air, pilot chutes out $1,500

Most of the dozens of flying circuses that made themselves a part of American life during the 1920s were unable to win themselves the kind of constant publicity that Ivan Gates seemed to be capable of generating as a matter of instinct. But none of his schemes won the Gates Flying Circus the kind of newspaper coverage its pilots and stunt men earned for it after a show girl named Rosalie Gordon—who had begged for the chance to make a parachute jump—found herself dangling helplessly from Pangborn's plane in the air over Houston's Ellington Field. Parachutists of the day fastened canvas cases containing their tightly folded chutes to one of a plane's struts while on the ground, climbed out on a lower wing and hitched themselves to the parachute after reaching a proper altitude, then pulled it free of its container by jumping into the air. Miss Gordon, however, was connected to one of these encased chutes by a length of rope as she sat in the cockpit before takeoff. A stunt man named Milton D. Girton climbed in with her.

Girton climbed out of the cockpit as they reached 2,000 feet and helped the young woman to the leading edge of the wing. Rosalie jumped without hesitation when they were correctly positioned over the field. But a loop of her rope, blowing about under the wing, became fouled in the landing gear. She fell 20 feet and hung in the wind under the plane: The lines of the chute, too, became entangled in the under-carriage. Girton scrambled down to the spreader bar between the landing wheels, but he could not pull the rope up, and Rosalie Gordon could not climb it. He scrambled back, as thousands watched in horror from the ground, to shout the details to Pangborn—who became suddenly aware that he had a perilously short supply of fuel.

Tommy Thompson flew his ship close beside Pangborn's with another stunt man, Freddy Lund, standing on his upper wing. Thompson slid his right upper wing tip under Pangborn's left lower wing. Lund jumped to Pangborn's plane and joined Girton on the landing gear. But the combined efforts of both men were not enough to budge the rope. Lund, who was slight of build, worked his way back to the rear cockpit, climbed in and took over the controls so Pangborn could climb out to lend his greater strength to the struggle on the landing gear.

Desperation at last begat success. Pangborn hauled the line up inches at a time, held it while Girton snubbed it against the spreader bar, gained a few more inches with another heave and finally—having pulled the stranded parachutist to within three feet of their perch—thrust one booted foot toward her. She seized his ankle with both hands. He strained to retract his leg. Girton got his hands under her shoulders and pulled her up to safety. Pangborn climbed, gasping, back to his cockpit and landed, with Milton Girton and Rosalie Gordon still sitting, precariously, on the spreader bar. The deed was celebrated in newspapers from coast to coast.

Those who decided to challenge fate by stunting in the air were not always so lucky. Wesley May—whose typically brief career provided a kind of ironic symbol of the developing role of the stunt men—sought employment during the infancy of the Gates circus after learning that a fellow daredevil, Thornton "Jinx" Jenkins, had narrowly escaped a fatal fall during a performance by hooking one ankle into a brace wire. May sent a telegram to Ivan Gates: WHEN PRESENT WINGWALKER IS KILLED, I WANT THE JOB.

Jenkins' chute failed to open during an exhibition at San Jose, California, a short time later, and May was duly hired. He rewarded his new employer with a brand new stunt: falling like a rock—while spectators screamed—before deploying one of the just-developed rip-cord parachutes. But May, too, soon came to grief. He unbuckled his parachute harness while making what he called the "Bullet Drop" during a show held near San Francisco and hung from the rigging by his hands as he neared the ground. He was blown away from the field after his parachute opened and came down in a cemetery shade tree, his parachute tangling in the foliage. He found himself standing on a branch, however, and relaxed his grip on the harness, just as the limb broke under his full weight. He fell on a tombstone, breaking his back. He was taken to a hospital—which he told visitors he would be leaving in a couple of days. He was dead before dawn.

"Colonel" Hubert Julian exuberantly calls attention to a Los Angeles billboard that advertises a 1931 performance of the Five Blackbirds, an all-black flying circus that Julian had founded. The billboard erroneously calls him "Rupert."

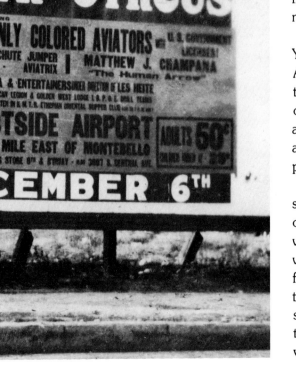

Ivan Gates was upset to find himself in possession of thousands of expensive and useless posters and lithographs bearing the names of Jenkins and May. "I'm sorry for Wes," he was quoted as saying, "but this death business is costing me money." Gates decided that wing-walkers would henceforth be considered replaceable laborers, like mechanics, and hit on the idea of billing May's successor as "Diavalo," an all-purpose name capable of reuse by other performers if fate were to remove any one of them from the show.

As Joe James settled into the circus routine of 1927 he was dazzled at meeting legendary pilots—and just as impressed to shake the hand of the man who had become the ultimate Diavalo, a cheerful Swede named Aaron Krantz. Krantz was not only daring and cheap—he worked as a mechanic between stunts, walked wings for $2.50 and performed parachute jumps for five dollars—but proved to be so durable that Gates eventually risked billing him as A. F. Krantz, World's Master Daredevil, on posters that identified him as the famous Diavalo. Years later, Krantz revealed that he had used "little secret devices" in creating some of his more spectacular effects. "I had a belt under my sweater that nobody could see and I had cables made up with snaps on them and hidden in the airplane. When I got up on the top wing I would hook the cables to the belt—nobody could see that I was snapping these fittings—and then stand up, stretch out good and tight, and the pilot would go into a loop."

Secret devices or not, Gates did not exaggerate in calling Krantz the Master Daredevil. "We had a trapeze that I attached to the landing gear with a mouthpiece and I used to go down and hang from that by my teeth," Krantz remembered. "Of course it had a big ball on the end that filled your entire mouth. I also used to slide back on the tail and stand on my head, and doing that I had no support at all."

Joe James's first performance for the circus was at the Greater New York Air Show, as Ivan Gates styled it, mounted at Teterboro Airport in August of 1927. The event inaugurated a series of hectic tours during the autumn of that year and the spring of 1928 by which time the Gates organization would reach its crest of profitability and prestige. Its pilots and stunt men, with the exception of James, were by now seasoned aerial circus veterans, intimately familiar with their routines, their airplanes and one another.

George Daws, a former New Orleans reporter, moved ahead of the show to place advertising and promote newspaper stories. So did a crew of roustabouts who marked the fields chosen for the next performance with lime to help the pilots spot them on arrival and illuminated them with buckets of gasoline set afire to guide planes in after dark. A small fleet of motor vehicles trundled from town to town: two-door flivvers for the advance men, a concession truck that sold hot dogs, soda pop and souvenirs as the fliers performed, a big touring car in which pilots were transported from airfields to local hotels and back again, and a moving van that served as a traveling billboard while hauling baggage, spare

Howard Hughes's air force for filming Hell's Angels —39 pilots, their mechanics and some of the 87 planes —is arrayed at Caddo Field, California.

parts and a suitcase often containing as much as $12,000 in cash collected at the last exhibition.

The most profitable efforts of Gates's death-defying aviators, however, still involved the transport of paying passengers. A barker-ticket seller beseeched the public to embrace the opportunity lest it elude them: "We will take you high or low, fast or slow, any way you care to go. It's worth a ride to see whether you like it or don't like it. Like Castoria, children cry for it and old maids sigh for it. The thrill of a lifetime! We will bring you down so gently even the grass won't object. Our pilots land as softly as an old maid getting into a feather bed. Fly over your house, see who's visiting your wife. We have special rides for mother-in-laws. Come on up and fly high with the angels."

Rides sold for five dollars, $2.50 and eventually, when the aircraft could carry four passengers at a time and passenger-handling on the ground became more efficient, for as little as one dollar. They lasted, on the average, no more than 90 seconds and involved exquisite precision flying by the pilots and a high degree of teamwork by the ground crew. The Standards had no brakes, but every flier was able to take off with two pairs of passengers facing each other, knee to knee, in his front cockpit, circle the field, touch down and come to a stop exactly beside a kind of corral into which waiting customers were herded after surrendering their money. Mechanics and roustabouts helped the plane's occupants out of the cockpit and down a metal ladder mounted on one side of the plane, while others pushed fresh passengers up a similar ladder on the other side of the fuselage.

The planes took off and returned with a kind of metronomic rhythm; where individual barnstormers averaged 25 passengers a week, Gates's pilots took hundreds aloft in a day; one of their number set an all-time record by carrying 980 passengers in one day. Pilots often landed while the next plane was still loading, and could gauge distance and control speed—sometimes by dramatic sideslipping—so accurately as to stop with their spinning propeller within a few feet of the tail of the plane ahead. Jack Ashcraft made a point of cutting his switch in flight, landing and coasting up to the corral with a dead engine—first blowing a bugle to attract the attention of those on the ground. The pilots continued the aerial merry-go-round as long as paying customers were available, pausing only to refuel and gulp down a sandwich before returning to the air.

Pilots began each day on tour with what they called the "morning bally" (for ballyhoo)—diving, looping and slow-rolling noisily over whatever town they were visiting to lure customers within range of the barker's persuasive bellow. Two or three fliers were directed to take off and perform similar stunts if the crowd showed signs of restlessness during the day; when sales of ride tickets flagged, the barker was authorized to summon Krantz from the tent in which he toiled as a mechanic and—after the stunt man had wiped his hands of grease and slipped into white ducks and a white jersey—send him aloft with Pang-

Stunt pilot Dick Grace slams his camouflaged plane into the ground at 105 mph while nearby cameras roll. Exploits like this one confirmed Grace's reputation as "the crash king of Hollywood."

born to restore the customers to an appropriate level of excitement.

"He will tamper with centrifugal force," the announcer bawled through a megaphone as Krantz climbed out on a wing. "He will defy gravity!" Krantz was starred again in an "evening bally" that closed each show. After such an exhausting routine, Joe James reported, "one's eyes become bleary and sightless, one's back is aching to the breaking point and the nerves are tied and tense in all sorts of fancy knots due to the constant strain." And still the planes had to be tied down and covered with tarpaulins for the night.

But the pilots were paid 20 per cent of the income received from passengers they carried aloft, plus 5 per cent of the gate receipts, and often, as James recalled, they sang at the top of their lungs on the way back to town. "I often wonder what the respectable people thought of us as we, in high tan riding boots, khaki breeches and leather jerkins, bronzed and black with dust and soot, would pull up to the entrance of the best hotel in town. No touring stock company with its painted women could have aroused more comment than the crazy eagles of the Gates Flying Circus."

Semiconscious, Grace sits in a German Fokker D.VII he has just wrecked for a scene in Wings. The next day he consulted a doctor to determine the extent of his injuries. His neck was broken.

But the crazy eagles and their World War I biplanes were the target of increasingly strident opponents by 1927. Local pilots and airport operators objected to the way circuses invaded their territories, skimmed off the cream of the aviation business, then left them to their year-round struggles to stay solvent. The Army Air Corps shut off a cornucopia of replacement aircraft and spare parts when it ordered the destruction of all Curtiss Jennies still in military service. And the Department of Commerce sought to tighten its control on civil aviation with increasingly rigorous regulations.

Many of these new rules struck directly at the most cherished practices of the circus. Planes were forbidden to fly within 300 feet of each other, to carry explosives or fireworks or to operate without navigation lights or from unlighted fields. Airplanes were subject to new standards and, if they did not meet them, were grounded by federal inspectors. One of these officials, Parker D. "Shorty" Cramer, had spoken bluntly to Gates in the spring of 1927 of the diminishing future of the circus. "We're going to make it safe for everyone to fly. The days of big flying circuses are over and we're going after the oldest, largest and best known first—this means you."

Gates ordered that the Standards be given newly overhauled Hisso engines and be painted at the repair shop near the Teterboro field. Government inspectors grounded them all, nevertheless—maintaining that planes built to carry two people could not legally carry five—while a crowd of 30,000 awaited their show at Providence, Rhode Island. Gates hired the original designer of the Standard, Charles Healy Day, who forced the government to back down by proving that the plane was fully capable of lifting the passengers who were being crammed into their enlarged forward cockpits.

But the Gates planes were grounded again in Johnstown, Pennsylvania, during their next tour in October. "We argued and stormed and pleaded," said James, and after hours of debate the government inspectors agreed to let at least Pangborn and Lee Mason fly. "The funny thing about it all," James said, "was that Mason's ship was the worst one in the outfit."

The running battle with the government continued. Gates refurbished the aircraft for the winter season and—heading south—requested a waiver permitting the performance of a plane change for a big Red Cross benefit show. The request was denied. Pangborn was grounded, after the circus's midwinter arrival in Florida, by an inspector who noticed that the flier had altered the top wing of his Standard. Other inspectors decided to cut holes in the fabric covering of circus planes to probe their underlying woodwork. Pangborn and his pilots objected vociferously, but the inspectors, backed by United States marshals, cut open the fabric nevertheless.

Crowds were bigger than ever as the circus headed through Ohio, Indiana and Pennsylvania in the spring of 1928, and the profits rolled in. But the aircraft were aging, the regulations tightening and the inspectors

Hollywood's air war

THE PILOTS IN *WINGS* DID THEIR BEST FOR CLARA BOW.

In the 1920s, Hollywood began to re-create the World War on film—especially the war in the air. Barnstormers-turned-stunt pilots flew mock dogfights over Southern California and other shooting locations, creating an image of war that seemed even more dramatic—and was certainly more romantic—than the real thing. In doing so they contributed to the legend of the World War I pilot as a chivalric, scarf-wearing fatalist who lived for today, because tomorrow he would die.

The best of the air epics were the best movies of their day. *Wings,* starring Richard Arlen and Buddy Rogers as the hero-pilots, in 1927 won the first Academy Award for Best Picture. A year later, Howard Hughes staked a fortune on *Hell's Angels.* When talkies, including Howard Hawks's *Dawn Patrol,* threatened to eclipse it, Hughes reshot *Angels* in sound to make it a box-office hit in 1930.

THE DAWN PATROL PREMIERED IN 1930 AND WAS REMADE IN 1938.

IT COST FOUR MILLION DOLLARS TO FILM *HELL'S ANGELS*.

more threatening than ever. Pilots began to desert to fly passengers and mail for the rapidly growing airlines. Ivan Gates too was involved with other enterprises. None concerned with the circus doubted that its days were numbered.

On the July Fourth weekend, veteran Gates pilot Bill Brooks demonstrated over Allentown, Pennsylvania, how superlative airmanship could compensate for even the worst equipment failure. A propeller blade (ironically, a new one-piece aluminum design) snapped off, unbalancing his engine so badly that it tore itself out of the airplane. Hopelessly tail heavy, the plane was condemned to a series of stalls. Brooks managed to keep the wings level through the descent, during which the plane would pitch forward, pick up speed, then pitch up in a full stall. He finally managed to pancake onto a street without injury to himself or his passenger.

On went the circus. It was grounded again in New Jersey, but drew one of the largest crowds of its history for an appearance in Providence. It returned to Teterboro Airport in October, having flown 273 exhibitions in 75 cities in 10 months, to find that Texaco had struck it a mortal blow; the company would no longer supply free fuel and oil.

Still more regulations were scheduled to take effect in 1929, barring from commercial use any aircraft whose design and performance had not been certified for manufacture after exhaustive testing. Clyde Pangborn decided that he too must abandon barnstorming for life as a commercial test pilot. Four remaining circus fliers—veterans Bill Brooks, Ive McKinney and Jack Ashcraft, and newcomer Homer Fackler—defied the inevitable and went on one last tour in November; they coursed through the Mississippi River states of Tennessee, Louisiana and Mississippi, with their aircraft still bravely displaying the Texaco insignia.

Ivan Gates and Clyde Pangborn were standing on the field among a growing crowd of mechanics and factory workers as this last squadron flew in wing to wing for a final landing at Teterboro. The four pilots executed five precision formation loops over the field and erupted into exhibitions of their best individual aerobatics, moving Gates to tears as they landed (Bill Brooks did one more loop and came in last). They taxied smartly into line, flipped back their goggles and cut their switches. The Gates Flying Circus had ceased to exist.

Thus ended the pioneering days of aerial entertainment, but not the flying circus itself. Only a year after the demise of the Gates organization, Jimmie and Jessie Woods of Wichita, Kansas, founded the most durable circus of all—one eventually called the Flying Aces. It performed continuously from 1929 through 1938.

The Flying Aces differed in two important ways from the Gates squadron. Jimmie and Jessie Woods bought new types of aircraft—Stearmans, Eaglerocks, Travel Airs and Swallows—and maintained strict control over their maintenance and overhaul. The Aces were a

Actor-aviator Reginald Denny (second from right) is welcomed by founder Bon MacDougall into the 13 Black Cats, a flamboyant company of Los Angeles-based stunt pilots who defied both superstition and the odds on survival.

self-contained, well-managed unit with a support staff of some 15 full-time people. They indulged in few of the flamboyant escapades that had characterized the Gates fliers, accommodated themselves more successfully to the burgeoning government regulations aimed at curtailing their activities, and operated profitably long after the Jennies, Standards and the flying gypsies spawned by World War I had disappeared from the scene.

Jimmie Woods managed the circus with a firm hand (a bed check made sure pilots were sober and asleep by midnight on any day preceding a show) and flew in almost every performance. His wife, Jessie, was the circus wingwalker, parachute jumper and surrogate mother. She became famous for sitting on the top wing of a Travel Air or Stearman while it was flown through barrel rolls, spins and loops. Her pet bulldog, Chandelle, became equally well known as ''The Flying Dog'' and logged a thousand hours of flight time.

He had competition. One of the Flying Aces was charged with round-

Jauntily perched between a truck and a trailer touting his motorcycle act, Rocky Moran (right) relaxes with his friend Parker Cunningham during a 1932 appearance of the Flying Aces Air Circus at Fond du Lac, Wisconsin. The versatile Cunningham was a stunt man, air-show announcer and advance booking agent.

Daredevil motorcyclist Rocky Moran crashes through a fiery barrier during a break between aerial exhibitions at the Fond du Lac airfield.

ing up a stray feline in every town, and the hapless animal, rechristened "Percival, The Educated Cat," was sent drifting to the ground from on high in its own miniature parachute—to be claimed, in most cases, by some fascinated spectator and lugged home to a life of ease. The Woods augmented such stunts with acts on the ground that were calculated to entertain audiences between acts in the air.

Clem Whittenbeck achieved national prominence in the 1930s with the Flying Aces for his inverted aerobatics, especially his breathtaking trademark pass over the flying field, upside down, at an altitude of about six feet, followed by an unbelievably rapid climbing turn, sideslip and landing back at center field.

The Flying Aces were not alone in the air. Millionaire sportsman Garfield Arthur "Gar" Wood financed a competing group, the Fordon-Brown National Air Show, which flew the best of new aircraft after its inception in 1937. Wood outfitted all the pilots in tailored uniforms and bought advertising with a lavish hand until he grew disenchanted by a disparity between income and outgo and killed the show by withdrawing his support.

There were still the government inspectors and regulations, of course, and even a circus that was as well organized and as conscientious as the Flying Aces felt burdened by the increasing weight of what they perceived to be governmental hostility. "They had so many rules," Jessie Woods recalled years later, "just choking us down. They got very nasty about us being there. They did not want air shows any more, we were too sensational. All they wanted then was to educate the people to the safety of flight and encourage the growth of business aviation and the airlines. What they did not realize was that there would not have been any airlines if there had not been people like us. We kept aviation before the eyes of the public and showed airplanes and flying to people all over the country who otherwise might not have even been aware that airplanes existed."

Federal regulations had tightened implacably by 1936. Wingwalking was permitted only above 1,500 feet, so high, as Jessie Woods exclaimed, that "no one could see it." Wingwalkers were further required to wear parachutes. Special fencing was mandated to contain crowds, and insurance requirements were drastically raised. Jimmie and Jessie Woods saw, like Ivan Gates before them, that it was futile to go on. They honored their contracts but began letting pilots go and disbanding their organization.

Congress, lobbied fiercely by representatives of the airlines, the aircraft manufacturers and the commercial fixed-base operators, was rewriting the regulations once more into the new Civil Aeronautics Act of 1938. Ivan Gates had died in despair, leaping from an apartment window in New York four years after the end of his circus. Many of his famous pilots had died in their cockpits. The flying circus, reminisced Joe James, "was grounded at last, its rickety old crates cracked up or unfit to fly, its pilots scattered or gone on their last flights."   ～

Mastering the art of precision flight

Aerobatic stunts by single planes or formations have dazzled crowds and satisfied the instinctive yearnings of the crack pilots who flew them ever since Peter Nesterov, an unsung lieutenant in the Imperial Russian Air Service, risked censure by looping the first loop in a Nieuport over Kiev on August 27, 1913.

More important, the knowledge acquired through aerobatics has contributed to the improvement of aircraft design and the refinement of flying skills. To meet the demands of rolls, loops, spins and stall turns, pilots and builders learned how to improve flight controls, tried to build the correct degree of stability and performance into the same plane, and developed practical techniques for training green aviators.

During World War I, the mastery of aerial acrobatics provided the basis for combat skills that became a matter of life and death for pilots forced into evasive tactics by enemy attackers. Courses such as Basic Battle Acrobacy were made mandatory for fighter pilots. In the early postwar years, aerobatics became largely the province of the barnstormers. Later, the air services of several nations organized elite exhibition teams whose close formation flying, refined to heart-stopping perfection, monopolized the public's attention at major air races.

Government safety restrictions eventually brought an end to the best days of the daredevil wingwalkers and plane-changers, but flying teams continued to perform and improve their high-speed sky ballets, demonstrating the skillful beauty of precision flight.

In a tight inverted formation, the United States Navy's Sea Hawks perform in Wasp-powered Boeing F-2Bs over Los Angeles as part of the 1928 National Air Races.

Flying almost as a mirror image, Paul Mantz maneuvers wheel to wheel beneath Frank Clarke at Oakland's 1938 Pacific International Air Races.

Cutting wires between two poles in 1939, Squeek Burnett demonstrates his talent for flying upside down as low as 12 feet from the ground.

Executing the spectacular chevron formation, the Italian Escadrille performs during an air meet at Château de Vincennes, France, in 1934.

3

The relentless quest for speed, speed, speed!

While rumpled troops of barnstormers and stunt men risked their necks capering through the skies in pursuit of a meager living and a measure of applause, another, quite distinct breed of airmen chased a different and even more perilous goal—sheer speed. The paths of these two groups often converged. Sometimes they came from the same flying schools, and often they participated in the same air shows, yet in spirit they were worlds apart. The barnstormers were essentially performers, the artists and daredevils of the air. The speed seekers considered themselves calculating men of science, advancing the frontiers of aviation technology by building and flying increasingly faster airplanes. They were men with a mission.

To be fastest, to couple the internal-combustion engine with the elusive properties of the perfect airfoil and press them both to the limit of their capacities—this was the challenge. The urge to possess the fastest airplane in the world became an obsession that enthralled the best technological minds of both Europe and America. In the United States, and then in England, France and Italy, the quest for speed was eventually underwritten by government treasuries and entrusted to the armed services. The great speed kings of the 1920s—notably Jimmy Doolittle in the United States, H. R. D. Waghorn in England and Italy's Mario de Bernardi—were all military men competing as much for national honor (and preparedness) as for personal glory. The planes they flew evolved rapidly from reconditioned war machines that buzzed along at 160 miles per hour to such engineering masterpieces as Italy's Macchi M.C.72, which in 1934 hit a speed of nearly 450 miles per hour—a record for a piston-engine seaplane that still stands.

A great part of the battle for speed was fought in wind tunnels and on the engine benches of mechanics and designers who repeatedly outdid themselves to create faster and more powerful machines. Most of the planes that served in World War I had been powered by what were essentially automobile engines. But through the ministrations of such men as Glenn Curtiss, Henry Royce and Mario Castoldi, the shape of the speed racers was streamlined and the engines became supremely complex power plants, with as many as 24 cylinders and generating more than 2,000 horsepower.

The great international air races were the lists in which the speed chasers put themselves and their machines to the test. Most of the early ones—the Pulitzer Trophy race, the James Gordon Bennett Cup, the

An Italian poster advertising the 1921 Schneider Trophy contest in Venice gives a lighthearted aura to the annual seaplane race, which actually was a hard-boiled competition among nations for supremacy in aeronautical engineering and design.

Beaumont Cup and the Coupe Deutsch de la Meurthe, offered a trove of cash and a trophy to the plane that could fly a designated course in the fastest time. Curiously, the most prestigious race of the period, for the Schneider Trophy, offered very little money to the victor—eventually none at all. The rules of the Schneider also seriously restricted the nature of the planes that could enter: Only seaplanes or flying boats could compete and, in order to qualify, each entry had to prove itself in a series of tests calculated to measure a quality that had little to do with aeronautics: seaworthiness.

Jacques Schneider, son of a French armaments manufacturer, came to manhood as the flying machine was beginning its first hesitant exploration of the air, and he threw himself with youthful enthusiasm— having first breathed the fumes of gasoline engines by racing fast motorboats—into the new age of aviation. Despite multiple arm fractures, which he suffered while powerboat racing in Monte Carlo, Schneider earned a pilot's license in 1911 and set a new national record by rising to 33,000 feet in a balloon.

Like many early aviators, he had his own peculiar vision of the future of flight. Schneider was irked by the practice of launching and landing

Maurice Prévost of France sits poised in the Deperdussin monoplane, fitted with twin floats, with which he won the first Schneider Trophy race, held at Monaco in 1913. Prévost was the only pilot who completed the 174-mile course.

airplanes from fields. His sense of logic told him that because so vast a proportion of the earth's surface was water and because its continents were so littered with lakes and rivers, pontoons or floats would surely make more useful landing gear than wheels.

In 1912, Schneider began a campaign to guide the infant aircraft industry along what he considered the path of reason. He began an international competition and personally donated its prize—the Coupe d'Aviation Maritime Jacques Schneider—to be awarded to the fastest "hydro-aeroplane" entered, until some aviation club won three times in a five-year span and gained permanent possession. The winning club each year would host the next year's race.

The Coupe was really not a cup at all; it was a silver sea wave, 22½ inches across, which was set on a marble pedestal. Recumbent in the wave were the figures of Neptune and his three sons; poised over them, and joined to the rest of the statuary solely by the eternal kiss she bestowed on one of the sea-god's sons, was the winged personification of the Spirit of Flight.

The huge classical trophy made an odd symbol indeed of the heated and often quarrelsome series of contests that were fought for it. The early seaplanes were temperamental creations, and the hydrodynamic problems involved in lifting such machines from the surface of the sea were only partially understood at the time.

Schneider's obsession with developing a seaworthy airplane was reflected in the rules he imposed. All entries were required to cover a distance of 547 yards "in contact with the sea." In later contests, they had to sit in the water for six hours to test the integrity of their hulls or pontoons and, in case of leaks, had to race—if still capable of doing so—without removing the accumulated liquid.

The conditions of the Schneider Trophy inspired innovative designs, and a number of displays of inadvertent farce. At the first competition for the trophy, held at Monaco in 1913, France's famed Roland Garros became a figure of comedy almost as soon as he opened the throttle of his Morane-Saulnier. The plane bounced on the wave tops like a bucking bronco, threw blinding sheets of spray over its own fuselage and then sloshed to a stop with a waterlogged engine. One Louis Gaudart suffered an even more ludicrous fate while trying to take off. His biplane engaged in a series of crazy, 10-foot jumps before sinking, nose first, like a startled mud hen. The pilot was not seen again.

Among the competing planes, the most promising was a blue Deperdussin piloted by a vitriolic Frenchman named Maurice Prévost. Just a year earlier, in 1912, a landplane version of the Deperdussin had become the first aircraft anywhere to reach a speed faster than 100 miles per hour on a straight course. Prévost's aircraft was a mid-wing monoplane—one of the first to use the revolutionary monocoque fuselage, a tapering tube of three-ply-tulipwood veneer wrapped around light lattice-like frames so that for the first time the outer skin of the aircraft was rigid enough to support itself. It was driven by the most advanced engine of the day, a 160-horsepower Gnôme rotary—the engine that, more than any other single factor, was responsible for France's domination of the early air races. The Gnôme was light and exceedingly reliable and it rarely overheated: Its 14 cylinders cooled themselves by spinning with the propeller around a fixed central shaft.

The course at Monaco, laid out over the Bay of Roquebrune, was four-sided and only 6.2 miles around. Each plane was to make 28 laps racing against the clock, with a staggered start. Prévost's powerful Deperdussin would have the edge on the long straightaways while lighter, more maneuverable planes, such as the American entry, a Nieuport flown by Charles Weymann, could take advantage of a particularly short leg near the harbor that required two rather sharp turns within a distance of just over 200 yards.

On the day of the race, the bay lay calm under a bright Mediterranean sun. Prévost started first, rising smoothly off the water and leveling out at about 50 feet. After five times around the course, he was averaging about seven minutes per lap. Weymann, who started about an hour after him, spent so much time getting airborne that it took him an unimpressive 18 minutes to complete the first lap. Once he was under way, however, he began to press Prévost. After 10 laps the Frenchman's lead was in serious jeopardy. After 15, Weymann was beating Prévost's time by three seconds, and five laps later the gap had widened to three minutes. The other two entries had by now dropped out of the race and, if he could maintain this margin for the last eight laps of the race, Weymann was certain to win.

Prévost had finished his laps and was anxiously watching Weymann's times as they were posted on a huge scoreboard overlooking Monaco's central harbor, when, to his surprise and the consternation of his fellow Frenchmen, it was announced that he had been disqualified. Jacques Schneider's complicated rules stipulated that the planes must fly across the finish line. Prévost had misread this section and had skimmed down 500 yards before the line and taxied across. He could, the judges informed him, take his plane back in the race and fly across the finish line, thereby assuring himself of second place. Prévost drew himself up in fine Gallic hauteur and flatly refused. His time, he pointed out, had been accumulating all the while; nothing would persuade him to recross the finish line now.

Well, almost nothing. For, at the height of this furor, Weymann's Nieuport, with only four laps to go, suddenly went silent and fell from the sky. The plane landed safely in the bay and boats were sent out immediately to tow Weymann into the harbor, where his mechanics anxiously waited. They were helpless, as it turned out. An oil line had burst, and the Nieuport would not fly again that day. Weymann was forced to withdraw from the race.

With this new development, Prévost's resolution dissolved. Amid the cheers of his countrymen, the Deperdussin roared off across the harbor, throwing up torrents of spray in its wake. Prévost circled the bay once

A triumph of handicapping

Spectators follow the 1925 King's Cup race on a scoreboard that shows the time each entrant arrives at a predetermined stopping point. As the event neared its finish, only three of 14 starters remained in contention, though five pilots were permitted to fly a special consolation race the second day.

Victory in Britain's annual King's Cup race, said one early winner, was likely to go to "the pilot whose equipment survived long enough for him to find his way with luck to the finishing point."

First staged in 1922 with a prize trophy donated by King George V, this endurance contest became the most prestigious—and the longest-lived—of English air races. Each plane was given a handicap, carefully calculated on previous performance, engine size and speed; starting times were then strung out over periods of up to four hours.

The handicappers proved their accuracy in the first race, a two-day event. After twice completing an 810-mile circuit of Great Britain, with two mandatory stops daily, the first five finishers landed within 45 minutes of one another, the winner and runner-up just two minutes apart. By 1926 the leaders were separated only by seconds at the finish.

Refinements in handicapping and yearly variations in stops, course length or number of circuits assured continued public interest in the King's Cup race, which in the 1930s was shortened to one day. The event continues to be run, the last of the great contests to survive from air racing's golden age.

and then zoomed across the finish line. The 58 minutes that were added to his total time as a result of the false finish brought his average speed down from 61 to 45 miles per hour. Prévost was declared the winner and presented with a check for 25,000 francs. Jacques Schneider's trophy would remain in France, at least for a year. But no sooner was the "flying flirt," as the trophy was eventually dubbed, ensconced at the headquarters of the Aero Club of France than plans were afoot across the English Channel to pry it loose.

In March of 1914, a tall young man named Thomas O. M. Sopwith stepped from the Paris boat-train at Victoria Station bent almost double by the weight of his luggage. Sopwith and an Australian named Harry Hawker had designed and built the body for a biplane—a light, exceedingly compact affair they called the Tabloid. They were betting that the Tabloid, married to the right engine and equipped with floats, would prove to be the fastest seaplane in the world. Gnôme still manufactured the world's premier airplane engine, and it was the latest model of the Gnôme extra-light rotary that Sopwith lugged off the train from Paris.

The match was felicitous. At Monaco in April, Sopwith's test pilot, Howard Pixton, swept past a field of entries from Switzerland, the United States and France (Maurice Prévost was there but was unable to coax his Deperdussin into the air from the unusually choppy sea) to win the trophy for Great Britain with an average time of 86.8 miles per hour. Pixton's performance was astounding. Just 50 or 60 feet past the starting line, the Tabloid seemed to leap from the water and roar off into the wind, banking around the first pylon with its wings almost perpendicular to the surface. Most seaplanes were handled quite cautiously at the time and nobody had seen one perform such antics. The rules of the race had been altered slightly that winter, requiring each plane to touch down at two points during its first lap. The length of time the planes were to remain in contact with the sea was left unspecified, so when Pixton swooped down and bumped his floats twice against the water's surface, hardly slackening his speed at all, the spectators, although mostly Frenchmen, burst into wild applause. The first lap, complete with touch-downs, took him only 4 minutes and 27 seconds—about half the best French time. By the last lap, the Tabloid had so outstripped the other entries that no one could doubt that T. O. M. Sopwith's new design was the shape of the future.

But no one in 1914 could have predicted the full extent of the war that was about to descend on Europe, or the protean changes that were in store for the airplane in the surge of technological advances that followed hard upon it. For four years the Schneider competition was suspended and the trophy remained in the possession of Great Britain's Royal Aero Club. During this period the winged Spirit's bottom grew shinier than the rest of the statuary, members of the club having fallen into the habit of patting it before hanging their hats on her feet. But the Schneider Trophy, for all such impertinences, continued to exert an increasing influence on aviation after the First World War.

It did so in large part because of an event that appeared to be completely unrelated to Jacques Schneider's dream of spawning commercially successful seaplanes—the development, by a self-educated American named Charles B. Kirkham, of the world's first wetsleeve-monobloc aircraft engine.

All the great water-cooled work-horse engines of the War—the early Hispano-Suiza, the Mercedes, the Rolls-Royce, the American-built Liberty—shared a deplorable tendency to overheat at high speeds. Mark Birkigt, the Swiss creator of the V-8 Hisso, went a long way toward solving this problem—and coincidentally achieving a new rigidity and lightness—by boring cylinders, into which were screwed steel liners, or sleeves, in a solid block of aluminum that was perforated with channels to allow the flow of water from a radiator.

Kirkham, chief engineer for the Curtiss Aeroplane and Motor Corporation, went a step further with his new K-12 engine. Not only was it a V-12 rather than a V-8, but its coolant flowed directly against the sleeves rather than through surrounding metal as in the Hisso. It was not, however, free of faults. Its oiling system often failed at steep angles of ascent and its cast aluminum block was porous enough to let precious water dribble from the cooling system when it was run for extended periods. John N. Willys, who had gained financial control of the Curtiss company in 1917, decided that there was no market for it and suspended production. Kirkham resigned in 1919 to found a firm of his own.

His legacy refused, however, to wither away. Willys sold the Curtiss aircraft business to Clement M. Keys, its wartime vice president, in order to concentrate on building automobiles. Keys, having seen a new 300-horsepower Hisso and having decided that the K-12—now slightly modified and called the C-12—was superior, gave an engineer named Arthur Nutt the task of eliminating its failings. Nutt's improved version, the CD-12 (CD for Curtiss Direct Drive), successfully endured a rigorous 50-hour test in 1921 and turned out 393 horsepower, or one horsepower for every one and a half pounds of engine weight (a quantum leap of efficiency from the standard Hisso's power-to-weight ratio of 1 to 2). Nutt installed the CD-12 in two experimental Navy pursuit planes while Keys cast about for the right place to test the new creation.

International airplane racing before the War had been conducted in a gentlemanly, if somewhat amateurish fashion by various aero clubs. But once the war-making properties of the airplane had been demonstrated, governments began financing the development of fast planes, and a kind of quasi-military struggle for ascendency sprang up. By 1920 at least four major contests offered prizes for the fastest airplane—the Schneider Trophy still preeminent among them—and, while many of the entries came from private airplane manufacturers, military pilots regularly competed and military observers almost always attended.

The major air-racing event in the United States, and the competition in which Nutt and Keys decided to try their new engine, was for the

Pulitzer Trophy, held first at Mitchel Field on Long Island in 1920 and at different airfields around the country in subsequent years. In setting up the contest, Ralph Pulitzer and his brothers, Herbert and Joseph Jr., publishers of the New York *World* and the St. Louis *Post-Dispatch,* had received the official approval of the United States government, and the American aviation industry was hopeful that this might inspire the government to give its financial backing to some of the more promising designs. Thus it was a surprise to nobody when, after Navy test pilot Bert Acosta sprinted the Curtiss plane past all other entries to win the race in 1921, both the Army and the Navy took an active interest in its development. During the next year, Nutt eliminated a few lingering bugs from the CD-12 and renamed it simply the D-12. The wetsleeve monobloc was indeed the master stroke that Kirkham had intended it to be. At the 1922 Pulitzer, planes powered by D-12s took the first four places. Henceforth, all international air racing would be contests among engines that were variations on its basic design. Keys, having proved his new engine in the Pulitzer, now turned his eyes toward Europe.

Apart from the Schneider Cup, the European air races at the time were relatively uninspiring affairs. The last of the Gordon Bennett Cup races, sponsored by the expatriate American publisher James Gordon Bennett, had been run in 1920 at the little French town of Étampes, just south of Paris. Although a series of fiascoes prevented all but two of the entries from finishing, the great French pilot Sadi Lecointe performed an impeccable display of speed flying in a Nieuport to win the race and give his country permanent possession of the Cup.

To carry on the French air-racing tradition—and assure Lecointe a stage for his talents—the widow of Henry Deutsch de la Meurthe, a wealthy French petroleum refiner who had been a moving force in competitive aviation before the War, instituted the Coupe Deutsch de la Meurthe, which came with a prize of 20,000 francs to be awarded to the winner. Unfortunately, the winner was not always the fastest plane entered. In 1921 and again in 1922 Sadi Lecointe, flying a Nieuport-Delage sesquiplane—a monoplane with an airfoil mounted between its wheel struts to provide additional lift—set new world speed records in the trials before the races and then proceeded to crash his planes during the actual competitions. After the 1922 event, in which only one of the entries succeeded in finishing the course, the Coupe Deutsch, much to the chagrin of spectacle-loving French enthusiasts, was suspended and never renewed.

Within a year, a millionaire named Louis Dudley Beaumont stepped in to fill the void. Beaumont, a transplanted American, invested 200,000 francs in the hope of promoting a race that would succeed where the Coupe Deutsch de la Meurthe had failed. The Aero Club of France agreed to manage the new event and chose a six-sided course near Istres as the scene of the contest. Sadi Lecointe and his backers at Nieuport set to work on a new 600-horsepower brute that was destined to be the only airplane ever to finish in competition for the Beaumont

The illustrious roster of Schneider winners

"It was a great victory, and our team are great men," wrote a patriotic observer of Great Britain's triumph in the 1927 Schneider Trophy race. Even the rival Italians cheered, he noted, when Britain's "three grimy heroes" climbed out of their cockpits.

More than any other air race, the Schneider could enshrine its winners and make them instant symbols of national aspiration. The strong emotional bond between Italy and its victorious 1926 team was expressed by the Air Minister, General Italo Balbo, who saluted the winners and then dropped a wreath of national mourning on the Lake Varese site where former team captain Vittorio Centurione had died in a crash during trophy trials.

For many victors, identified here with their winning aircraft and speeds for every year the trophy was contested, the race remained the high point of their careers. In 1959, when the distinguished airman Mario de Bernardi was found dead of a heart attack in his plane after stunt-flying over Rome, news accounts of his achievements all reached back to the sunny day at Hampton Roads, Virginia, 33 years before, when he had captured the Schneider Trophy for Italy.

1913: MAURICE PRÉVOST (Fr.)
Deperdussin
45.71 mph

1914: HOWARD PIXTON (Br.)
Sopwith Schneider
86.83 mph

1920: LUIGI BOLOGNA (It.)
Savoia S.12
105.97 mph

1921: GIOVANNI DE BRIGANTI (It.)
Macchi M.7bis
117.85 mph

1922: HENRI BIARD (Br.)
Supermarine Sea Lion II
145.72 mph

1923: DAVID RITTENHOUSE (U.S.)
Curtiss CR-3
177.27 mph

1925: JAMES DOOLITTLE (U.S.)
Curtiss R3C-2
232.57 mph

1926: MARIO DE BERNARDI (It.)
Macchi M.39
246.49 mph

1927: SIDNEY WEBSTER (Br.)
Supermarine S.5
281.65 mph

1929: HENRY WAGHORN (Br.)
Supermarine S.6
328.63 mph

1931: JOHN BOOTHMAN (Br.)
Supermarine S.6B
340.08 mph

Cup. After Lecointe won the race by default in 1924 and again in 1925—the other entries either were forced down or failed to take off—the Aero Club of France declared the contest closed; Beaumont returned to America a disenchanted Francophile.

Despite such attempts to set up alternatives, the Schneider Trophy remained the greatest challenge to aviators in postwar Europe. For all its annoying regulations and the fact that it was restricted to seaplanes and flying boats, the Schneider had grown more prestigious with each year. In the first run for the trophy after the War, an Italian pilot named Guido Janello bravely steered his plane through a dense, enshrouding fog at Bournemouth, England, and crossed the finish line—the only plane still in the race. The coveted trophy was not to be his, however. The Royal Aero Club had anchored a reserve mark boat, which duplicated its three official mark boats, in a little cove to the southwest of the starting point. Janello had rounded this false marker rather than the true one, a boat anchored in a similar cove not far away.

The decision disqualifying Janello was greeted with cries of rage and accusations of perfidy by the Italian delegation and with disbelief by Janello—who had set off on an extra lap for good measure and had suffered for it by running out of fuel and drifting about in the fog until finally located and towed to shore. Italian sensibilities were only partially soothed when the Fédération Aéronautique Internationale, which controlled the contest, invited the Royal Aero Club of Italy to manage the next year's race.

Both the 1920 and 1921 Schneider Trophy races were held at Venice. For a variety of reasons, all the foreign entries were forced to drop out of the competition in both years. Thus, Italy raced unopposed, taking the trophy with flying boats that floated on their fuselage-hulls, first a Savoia S.12 flown by Lieutenant Luigi Bologna and then a Macchi M.7 flown by Giovanni de Briganti. Although there was no chance to compare them with seaplanes, which sat off the sea on pontoon landing gear, the Italian flying boats were immensely impressive machines—swift, powerful and remarkably immune to rough weather.

Italy would no doubt have won permanent possession of the trophy with a third victory by default the following year had not the British appeared in Naples with the only non-Italian entry in the race: Supermarine Aviation Works' Sea Lion II. Henri Biard, its pilot, milked every drop of speed from its outdated hull, mounted with a 450-horsepower engine donated by Napier, and squeezed out a narrow victory over the Italian entries. The race made sensational news all over Europe, and once more the Schneider Trophy was the most sought-after trinket in the race for speed in the air.

Its gleam was so bright that it caught the eyes of Clement Keys and the officers of the United States Naval Bureau of Aeronautics, who were eager to test the mettle of their now nearly perfected Curtiss D-12 engine. The Navy took the first step. It decided in early 1923 that the development of seaworthy fighter planes could be stimulated by seeking the Schneider Trophy; it forthwith asked the recently formed National Aeronautic Association to enter four Navy planes in the event: two Curtiss racers powered by D-12's, a Navy Wright biplane and a reconditioned Navy fighter called the TR-3A. The race was to be held in September at Cowes, on the Isle of Wight off England's south coast.

Four pilots were chosen in June: Lieutenants David Rittenhouse, Rutledge Irvine, Adolphus Worthington "Jake" Gorton and Frank "Spig" Wead. Although they were already crack pilots, all four were put through an intensive, summer-long period of training in seaplanes. The pilots and their mechanics sailed for England in August on board the liner *Leviathan*—the aircraft being simultaneously dispatched in a cruiser—and at Cowes they began a final month of rigorous preparation for the race. They suffered one calamitous setback: The engine of the Navy Wright plane blew up at the conclusion of a trial run and the plane

At speeds up to 181 mph, Lieutenant David Rittenhouse wins the 1923 Schneider Trophy race at Cowes in his Curtiss CR-3 Navy racer, eliciting a cheer from a launch full of Americans (left).

was wrecked beyond repair, although Gorton, who hit the water at 200 miles per hour, was picked up unhurt by a fishing boat.

On race day, the Americans made it dramatically clear that the Curtiss racers were far superior to any aircraft yet produced in Europe, not to mention the Navy's own TR-3A, which never got off the water. England's lone entry, the same Supermarine Sea Lion that had won the trophy in 1922, had been fitted with a more powerful engine and achieved nearly 160 miles per hour. A French flying boat was forced to set down with engine trouble before completing the race. But Rittenhouse and Irvine, who took off together and raced each other around the triangular course, snarled through lap after triumphant lap while sailors on board the U.S.S. *Pittsburgh*—anchored off Cowes to lend them moral support—cheered madly every time they flashed by. Rittenhouse won the trophy with an average speed of 177.279 miles per hour. Irvine finished second at 173.347.

The Americans were applauded warmly enough by Englishmen who

Jimmy Doolittle streaks to victory at the controls of a Curtiss R3C-2 seaplane in the 1925 Schneider race held near Baltimore.

gathered along miles of beaches and on yachts clustered off Cowes, but there were those among their hosts who felt there was something unsporting in the methodical zeal the United States had displayed in preparing for the race. Everything, as one magazine writer noted, had been tailor-made for the job, from the steerable landing trolleys to the waders the men wore. *The Times* commented: "British habits do not support the idea of entering a team organized by the State for a sporting event."

But after the 1923 race, British habit, *The Times* notwithstanding, did an abrupt about-face. Both Italy and England reacted to defeat by buying several Curtiss engines in an effort to plumb the secret of America's success. While the Italians simply sent a pair to its Fiat works for testing, the British Air Ministry delivered one to Rolls-Royce (quietly, because of chauvinistic grumbling in Parliament) with specific instructions: Build a copy that would outperform the original. Rolls engineers did so with a vengeance, using the Curtiss wetsleeve-monobloc concept not only in a new R (for racing) engine but, eventually, in building the famed Merlin that powered Britain's fighter aircraft in World War II. All of this, however, took time. England and Italy were the beneficiaries that next autumn of a sporting gesture by the Americans, who called off the Schneider race of 1924 to give the Europeans time to build new planes.

When, in 1925, the Europeans did come to the United States to try to retrieve the Schneider Trophy, they were brimming with hope. The Italians, betting on rough water in Chesapeake Bay, stuck stubbornly to flying boats with two new Macchi M.33s. Both British entries—a Supermarine monoplane, the S.4, and a Gloster III biplane—sat, by contrast, on floats and were powered by a new engine, a Napier Lion of 700 horsepower, capable of driving a plane at speeds in excess of 200 miles per hour. Rolls-Royce was still perfecting its wetsleeve monoblocs.

"Never," said the English magazine *Flight,* "have we tackled an international speed race in so thorough a manner." But to little avail. The Supermarine S.4 pancaked into the sea and sank, the victim of aileron flutter during a high-speed trial, though not without allowing its pilot, Henri Biard, to swim to the surface alive. In the race itself the Gloster III averaged 199.16 miles per hour, exceeding the performance of the Macchi flying boat by 30 miles per hour and outlasting two Curtiss R3C-2 United States Navy racers. But the Gloster finished only second for all that.

A third R3C-2 performed faultlessly for the Army's Lieutenant James Harold "Jimmy" Doolittle—a stranger to hydroplanes but a man of unusual intellectual and physical capacities who was rapidly proving himself one of the great aviators of all time. Doolittle, willing to endure more punishment than most pilots, rounded the pylons almost vertically at full throttle and not only retained the trophy for the United States but broke all the world's closed-circuit records for hydroplanes as he did so. Doolittle averaged 232.57 miles per hour for the 217-mile race.

No one, it appeared, could match the American seaplanes. Yet at just that point, the Americans lost interest in the quest for speed. Perhaps it was because the American aircraft establishment was turning to the more profitable development of transport planes, or because many in Congress—which controlled the funding for such experimental aircraft —felt that racers of the day were approaching the practical limits of speed. The Americans were committed to defend the Schneider Trophy again in 1926, but the federal government made it clear that public money would no longer be spent on winning the competition.

The United States would enter slightly refurbished versions of the same three R3C-2s they had raced in 1925. The Italians, for their part, were so confident of recapturing the trophy that they assumed the Americans were just trying to save their money. After all, Italy's imperious dictator, Benito Mussolini, had decreed that the Schneider Trophy be won by Italy in 1926 no matter the difficulties to be overcome.

Thus, with America taking a back seat, the world looked to England and Italy for the seaplanes that would achieve a new speed record. Two men, Reginald Joseph Mitchell of England's Supermarine Aviation Works, Ltd., and Mario Castoldi, chief designer of Aeronautica Macchi, were pitted against each other in the race to build the winning plane.

Major Mario de Bernardi waves confidently from his cockpit after finishing a trial run of the 1926 Schneider Trophy course at Hampton Roads, Virginia. The Italian's stunning triumph two days later dashed American hopes of retiring the trophy with a third consecutive victory.

Mitchell, the son of a Yorkshire printer, was a quiet man, even shy at times, who listened patiently and intently to the ideas of his associates and was able to weave disparate suggestions into brilliant syntheses. As chief designer at Supermarine, he nursed an almost pathological concern for fliers who tested his airplanes. He wore swimming trunks while watching the trial of his S.4 from a launch in the hope of being able to rescue pilot Henri Biard in case of difficulty. He was shaken when the plane went down over Chesapeake Bay in 1925—but not so shaken as to believe he could not produce something faster and safer in the future.

Mitchell's Italian rival was a worthy adversary but a very different sort of man. Mario Castoldi was a jealous guardian of his own concepts. He kept them secret even from close associates and went so far as to produce false drawings in the hope of leading competitors into error. His task in 1926 was complicated by the need to abandon the central hull around which all former Italian racing hydroplanes had been built and to turn, like the British and Americans, to floats. He did so by a frantic process of borrowing and innovation.

Castoldi had watched the races of 1925 at Chesapeake Bay and had inspected the airplanes that beat his flying boats. It took him only a few days to produce the basic outlines of a racing monoplane that followed the British and American formula of a streamlined fuselage sitting above the water on two floats. Tranquillo Zerbi, Fiat's famed engine designer, augmented Castoldi's efforts, meanwhile, by building a new 12-cylinder racing engine. It was modeled closely on the Curtiss D-12, but Zerbi added ideas of his own—particularly an ingenious use of magnesium alloys—and was rewarded by achieving 882 horsepower in bench tests at the factory. The first of four scarlet Macchi M.39s (Castoldi numbered his racing aircraft with multiples of 13 for good luck) was ready for trials in mid-September, only eight months after conception, and broke all seaplane records by reaching nearly 260 miles per hour. But this new breed of racers was tricky to fly. Propeller torque caused the planes to lean dangerously during takeoff runs, and their unusually large floats made them hard to control once aloft.

Shortly after arriving at Hampton Roads, Virginia, in October 1926, one of the Macchi engines caught fire during a trial run. Castoldi chose to believe he was the victim of sabotage and demanded that the Italian planes henceforth be supplied fuel from the same tanks that supplied the American planes. But the engine of yet another M.39 hammered itself into junk after breaking a connecting rod—and failed again during the race itself after a crew of Italian mechanics had labored without sleep to rebuild it in time for takeoff.

To Italy's advantage, Mitchell had been unable to finish his new Supermarine in time for the race, and no British entries were present. Curtiss, however, without any military funding, had added 100 horsepower to the engine of one of the United States Navy's 1925 R3C-2s, and the upgraded machine posed a substantial threat.

Italy's top flier, Major Mario de Bernardi, flying one of the remaining

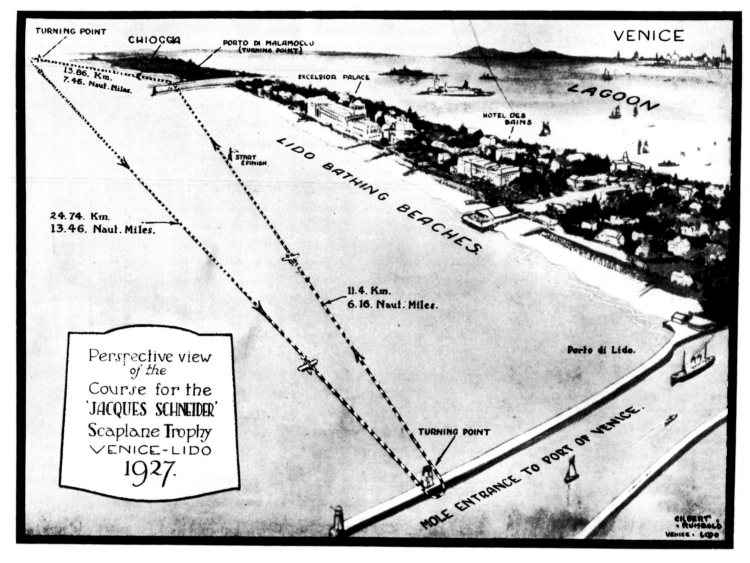

The characteristic three-cornered course of the Schneider race is traced in this map from a British aviation magazine's preview of the 1927 competition. To complete the contest, a pilot had to make seven circuits of the triangle, whipping his plane sharply around the turning points.

Macchi M.39s, set the pace in the race, despite having to climb to 600 feet to cool an overheating engine. He outraced the United States Navy's Lieutenant George Cuddihy—whose plane quit with a broken fuel pump within sight of the finish line after running only a few miles per hour slower than de Bernardi's M.39—and won the trophy. De Bernardi wasted no time in sending Mussolini a triumphant cable: YOUR ORDERS TO WIN AT ALL COSTS HAVE BEEN CARRIED OUT.

But the 1926 Schneider Trophy race marked more than a glorious hour for Italian aviation. For the first time, the speed of a seaplane—the Macchi had averaged 246.496 miles per hour—was approaching that of the record-holding landplane: 278.47 miles per hour achieved by the French pilot Florentin Bonnet in a Bernard monoplane at the Istres airdrome in 1924.

Italy, and the rest of the world, awaited the 1927 race with anticipation while the firms of Rolls-Royce, Supermarine, Fiat and Macchi strove to create the winning machine. A noisy throng invaded Venice during late September to watch de Bernardi and three other Italian

Racegoers wade ankle-deep for a better view of the Schneider Trophy race above the crowded Lido at Venice in 1927. British Flight Lieutenant S. N. Webster won the race after three identical Italian planes were forced out by mechanical failures.

pilots, flying Macchi M.52s, defend the Coppa Schneider against a new but essentially conservative S.5 monoplane that Mitchell had designed for England, and a new Gloster biplane. (The United States, for the first time since 1923, was not represented.) Two hundred thousand people stood shoulder to shoulder along the Lido as the planes warmed up. But Italy's racing fortunes, as things turned out, had reached their apogee at Hampton Roads. All the Italian engines—superhigh-compression power plants from which Fiat attempted to extract 1,000 horsepower—broke down during the race. Two Royal Air Force pilots, Flight Lieutenants S. N. Webster and O. F. Worsley, finished first and second—with Webster averaging 281.65 miles per hour—by wringing the last possible revolutions from beefed-up versions of England's dated but dependable Napier Lion VII-B engine.

Five weeks after the race, Mario de Bernardi had one of the Macchi M.52s officially clocked at an incredible 297.83 miles per hour certifying that the Schneider racers, with their clumsy-looking floats and their aeronautically useless watertight qualities, were the fastest-moving machines in the world, bar none.

One of the explanations for this remarkable achievement was that the vast, flat launching field offered by the water's surface allowed seaplanes to make long takeoff runs; they could thus build up enormous speed and lift themselves into the air with extremely short wingspans that created less drag and consequently allowed more speed. Another factor (not fully understood at the time) was that the long missile-shaped floats that everyone found so awkward were actually more streamlined than the conventional, nonretractable landing gears on the landplanes. Winning Jacques Schneider's trophy was now indisputably the most distinguished accomplishment in aviation.

After the race of 1927, it was agreed—with the awesome problems of design in mind—that the trophy would henceforth be contested only every other year. Even so, both Italy and England found they had scant time to cope with the difficulties of achieving just the proper propeller shapes, or mixing the right proportions of gasoline, benzol and tetraethyl lead for new, temperamental high-compression engines. The Italians—goaded by Mussolini's ambitious Air Minister, General Italo Balbo—reacted, nevertheless, with a kind of technological impetuosity. Isotta-Fraschini engineers developed 1,800 horsepower in an 18-cylinder engine and Mario Castoldi produced the seaplane—Macchi M.67 (this time, Castoldi pointed out, his numbers added up to 13)—that received the multipistoned brute engine.

Mitchell proceeded in England along a more cautious line, achieving speed in small increments through small changes. For his new plane, the S.6, he lengthened the fuselage of the S.5 by two feet and the wingspan by three. But there was no squeezing more power from the aged Napier Lion engine. Like Castoldi, Mitchell needed horsepower in fresh torrents. He got it from Rolls-Royce.

Henry Royce—now an old man who walked with a cane—bridled at the kind of thinking that had prompted Isotta-Fraschini to seek extra power through the dogged addition of extra cylinders. He sat on a beach near his home with three Rolls engineers and drew the outlines of the R engine in the sand with his stick. It should, he said, remain a V-12, should incorporate (with improvements) the concepts built by Kirkham into the Curtiss wetsleeve monobloc but should not flirt with the kind of ultrahigh compression used by the Italians. The needed quart of power would be extracted from a pint pot by a supercharger—a mechanism that would force more air-fuel mixture into the cylinders than atmospheric pressure would normally admit. The first model was completed in May of 1929; it produced 1,545 horsepower at 2,750 rpm's—and began chewing up its own vital organs in 15 minutes.

The townspeople of Derby, site of the Rolls plant, were subjected to endless days of hideous noise as the summer wore on. Thirteen times the modified engines failed. But on the 14th try, the R ran for 100 minutes at 1,850 horsepower. The first of Mitchell's S.6s was lowered into the water off Calshot Castle, near Portsmouth, on August 5.

Under the watchful eye of designer Reginald J. Mitchell (right), a team of British mechanics works over one of Mitchell's Supermarine S.6 racers on the night before the 1929 Schneider Trophy contest. The plane was ready by starting time and went on to win the race for England.

The Italians—at a point in August when they should have been preparing to leave for England—were having difficulties of their own. Only one of three Macchi M.67s was ready for testing; it reached 362 miles per hour in a trial run over Lake Garda, then suddenly dived into the lake, killing its pilot, Captain Guiseppe Motta. It was assumed that engine fumes may have entered the cockpit, and ventilating tubes were installed in the two remaining M.67s. Both, however, were yet untried, and General Balbo announced—after the Royal Aero Club refused to grant a postponement—that "the Italian team is going to England merely to perform a gesture of chivalrous sportsmanship."

The race was held on a glorious late-summer day and more than a million people crowded together on yachts, on the decks of H.M.S. *Iron Duke,* on ocean liners pressed into service as excursion steamers, at Calshot Castle and along beaches. Two of the three Italian fliers, Lieutenants Remo Cadringher and Giovanni Monti, gave the spectators demonstrations of high personal bravery as well as the sportsmanship to which General Balbo had alluded: Both, it quickly became apparent, were risking their lives by flying the untried Macchi M.67s.

The M.67s were wickedly beautiful aircraft and Cadringher's ship seemed challenger enough as he sent it screaming into the 33-mile course. But smoke and fumes from the plane's exhaust pipes were blown into the cockpit on the first turn, and the ship skidded wildly as the pilot, half-blinded, fought the controls while choking. He recovered while on the verge of a high-speed spin and found himself tearing inland before he could turn back into the course. Cadringher managed, miraculously, to complete a lap, averaging 284 miles per hour, but he landed shortly thereafter on finding himself unable to see the pylons through his smoke-hazed windscreen.

Monti did better, averaging 301.5 on his first circuit, but as he turned into the second lap a pipe in his radiator system burst, scalding his arms and legs with boiling water and filling his cockpit with steam. Still, he was able to touch down at better than 100 miles per hour to await rescue and removal to a hospital.

Mitchell's two new S.6s behaved, by contrast, with utter docility, snapping through lap after lap amid an uproar of applause from the great crowd. Flight Lieutenant H. R. D. Waghorn averaged 328.63 miles per hour in one plane, Flying Officer R. L. R. Atcherley 325.54 in the other, although he was forced to relinquish second place when the judges ruled that he had cut a pylon in the first lap.

"We have finished playing our part as sportsmen," said General Balbo at a post-race banquet. "Tomorrow our work as competitors will begin." Italian hopes for victory in 1931 centered once more on Castoldi and Macchi. Castoldi had high hopes of success at last after Fiat developed an engine with two contrarotating propellers to ensure gyroscopic balance and cancel out the lopsided takeoffs due to prop torque. The M.C. (for Macchi-Castoldi) 72—a sleek dragonfly of a plane he designed around this engine—reached 375 miles per hour in early trials

While a racing seaplane roars low overhead, spectators jam an English beach to watch the 1929 Schneider Trophy contest.

but crashed only a little later and killed the heroic Giovanni Monti. The Italians petitioned for a further postponement of the race.

The English, with only one more race between them and permanent possession of the trophy, were in no mood to grant special dispensations. Both Italy and France (a French entry under construction was not ready either) were forced to withdraw, and England had only to send one plane around the course to win the trophy, which the members of the Royal Aero Club—who now called it the "hatrack"—had grown quite fond of. But England's chances of doing so in style might well have suffered badly—the Air Ministry having refused, after 1929, to spend another shilling on racing—had it not been for the rich widow of a shipping millionaire who was delighted to put up the money for new planes and engines in order to castigate England's Labor government for "the poisonous doctrine that we are a third-rate power."

"I am proud," announced Lady Lucy Houston, "to say I inherit the spirit of my forefathers, who considered one Englishman equal to any three foreigners. We are not worms to be trampled under the heel of Socialism but true Britons with a heart for any fate!"

True to Lady Houston's portrayal, the English were not about to skulk off with the trophy without ending the years of demanding Schneider competition on a properly dramatic note. All believed, before the Italian withdrawal, that speeds approaching 400 miles per hour would be needed to win the race, and they aimed their sights intently toward that mark. Rolls-Royce engineers went to work and extracted 2,350 horsepower from a successor to the R engine without appreciably increasing the weight of the 1929 engine of 1,850 horsepower. There had been grumblings in Italy and France that the English were equally unprepared and were about to take the trophy on a bluff, but Mitchell was confident that his new airplane, the Supermarine S.6B, would silence such talk.

The race, which had been scheduled for the second Saturday in September 1931, had to be postponed a day due to dirty weather, but the following morning dawned bright and fine. Nearly a million proud Englishmen jammed the coast around Portsmouth and the Isle of Wight, sensing—despite the absence of competition—that history was to be made that day.

The Supermarine S.6B, its aluminum hull painted blue and silver with red, blue and white tail stripes, was nudged off its barge near Calshot Castle, and a young flight lieutenant named John N. Boothman climbed into the cockpit behind the two splayed humps of cylinder banks on the big V-12 engine. Running at the speed at which Boothman expected to drive it, the engine would last for between 40 and 90 minutes before it started to melt on its mounts. Even an ingenious cooling system involving five long fluted tubes that could be seen running down the sides of the fuselage could not keep so thunderous a monster cool for long. The engine, in fact, had never been test-flown for longer than 27 minutes, and Boothman was hoping it would not take

The patriotic Lady Lucy Houston, who put up $453,000 to support Britain's 1931 Schneider Trophy bid, is greeted by team captain A. H. Orlebar as she arrives at Calshot for the race. "Every true Briton would rather sell his last shirt," she declared, "than admit that England could not afford to defend herself."

Capping his victory with a flourish, Flight Lieutenant John Boothman circles over the heads of spectators at Calshot Castle after having captured the 1931 Schneider Trophy. With Boothman's victory, Britain had won the competition three times in succession, and thus took permanent possession of the coveted trophy.

him too much longer than that to complete the seven 33-mile laps of the triangular course.

At 1:02 p.m., the S.6B planed off the choppy sea in a wall of spray and streaked around the first lap in just five and one half minutes, averaging 343.1 miles per hour. As he banked into a turn over the town of West Wittering, Boothman was able to see Henry Royce's home and the beach where his R engine had first been conceived. His instrument panel was now registering a speed of nearly 380 miles per hour in the straightaway.

The next six laps were stunning repetitions of the first, averaging 342.7, 340, 338.3, 339.6, 339.4 and 337.7 miles per hour. By the last lap, the Supermarine was listing badly to the left—probably because of the change in the plane's trim as fuel was consumed. But the end was near, and as Boothman crossed the finish line with a deafening roar, he swooped skyward in a final triumphant ascent. The wall of spectators, two miles long, burst forth in uncontrollable applause amid a happy cacophony of steamship whistles and bells. The race had taken only 47 minutes and the average speed had been 340.08 miles per hour; the Supermarine was indisputably the fastest airplane in the world.

Thus ended Schneider Trophy racing—but not its influence on the future of aviation. Boothman's performance was augmented and the work of Mitchell and Rolls-Royce was further dramatized later that same month. Flight Lieutenant George H. Stainforth became the first man in the world to break the 400-mile-per-hour barrier. His plane was Boothman's S.6B racer, for which Rolls had prepared a sprint engine capable of producing 2,600 horsepower. Stainforth averaged 407.5 miles per hour, hitting 415.2 at one point, during five 1.9-mile runs over Southampton Water.

Mario Castoldi's flair for design and his passionate involvement in Schneider Trophy races also was rewarded at last: Warrant Officer Francesco Agello, a tiny veteran racing pilot, flew one of Castoldi's M.C.72s at 440.68 miles per hour—a piston-engine hydroplane record that was never to be eclipsed—in the autumn of 1934.

The pressures of competition had wrought astonishing advances in aircraft performance. Ten years of development in engine design, said A. F. Sidgreaves, managing director of Rolls-Royce, had been collapsed into two years through research for the Schneider Trophy.

It was Mitchell, however, who made the most of the Schneider Trophy experience. He rebelled at the British Air Ministry's increasingly restrictive view of pursuit aircraft and talked his fellow directors into taking a chance on the production of an advanced fighter plane as a private venture. He then spent the declining months of his life—having discovered in 1935 at the age of 40 that he was dying of cancer—in translating the aerodynamic characteristics of his racing planes into the fighter plane that would almost singlehandedly save England from invasion, the Supermarine Spitfire of World War II.

Dole's ill-starred derby

On the heels of Charles Lindbergh's celebrated flight to Paris, pineapple tycoon James D. Dole tried to lure the young hero into making additional history in the opposite direction. He offered a $35,000 purse for a race, in August 1927, from California to the Hawaiian Islands. Lindbergh declined to enter—the first of a series of anticlimaxes, disappointments and tragedies that were to mar the event.

In June the race was shorn of any historic aspect when a pair of United States Army aviators in a Fokker Trimotor became the first to fly from the mainland to the islands. Then, of the 15 eager aviators who accepted Dole's challenge, three were killed in crashes while getting ready for the race. One plane was disqualified after its instruments were found to be wildly inaccurate, another when it was calculated that its fuel would run out 200 miles short of Hawaii. The eight planes that managed to qualify, all single-engined craft, were perilously overburdened with fuel—and most were undersupplied with good sense.

Among the entrants were some of the best-known barnstormers and stunt pilots of the day (and one nonflier, 22-year-old schoolteacher Mildred Doran, who was a passenger in a plane bearing her name). But many of the pilots seemed unaware that crossing 2,400 miles of Pacific Ocean and then finding a pinpoint of land was no casual undertaking. Most had little or no experience in overwater navigation and only a few—among them Hollywood stunt man Art Goebel—knew anything about instrument flying. Most engaged navigators—of varying degrees of skill—to accompany them.

Only four of the eight qualifying planes managed to get out of sight of land. Two of the others crashed on takeoff (the fliers survived); one pilot turned back because of engine trouble, and another quit when the wind began shredding the fabric skin from his plane. Art Goebel won the race; his Travel Air monoplane, the *Woolaroc,* landed at Wheeler Field outside Honolulu on the morning of August 16. He was followed two hours later by barnstormer Martin Jensen in a Breese monoplane, the *Aloha.* The other two planes that had set out from Oakland, the *Miss Doran* and the *Golden Eagle,* were never seen again.

Spectators and automobiles border the field at Oakland Municipal Airport, where the Oklahoma (left), first plane to take off in the Dole race, is poised at the starting line. Its flight was aborted by engine trouble.

In the sequence at left, El Encanto (The Enchanted), second plane to start in the Dole Derby, lurches to one side and crashes on takeoff. Its crew was unhurt.

The overloaded Pabco Pacific Flyer, third to the starting line, lifts off briefly; moments later it stalled and crashed. The wreck of El Encanto is visible in the background.

A newsreel cameraman records the takeoff of Martin Jensen's *Aloha*, the sixth plane to attempt the start and only the second to make a successful departure. The first plane that managed to get off, a Lockheed Vega piloted by Jack Frost, was one of those lost in the Pacific.

Arms raised in triumph, Art Goebel receives a winner's welcome at Wheeler Field after crossing from Oakland to Honolulu, with the help of radio beacons, in 26 hours 17 minutes 33 seconds.

4

The ultimate extravaganzas of high-stakes racing

The man portraying Adam plodded through the August heat of the downtown streets of Cleveland, Ohio, draped in a tiger skin. Behind him stretched three miles of marching units, bands and 100 floats depicting in fresh flowers the history of transportation, upward from Adam's feet through oxcarts and automobiles to the ultimate in technical progress—the airplane. Eighty thousand people, packed densely along the five-mile route, jostled for a clear view. In the sky overhead, squadrons of wheeling aircraft and sedate blimps escorted the parade on its way. When the man wearing the tiger skin reached the municipal auditorium complex just off Cleveland's central square, the 1929 National Air Races and Aeronautical Exposition were under way.

The exposition site at the auditorium boasted 320 exhibits including more than 100 aircraft. On the first afternoon alone, some 45,000 people came to marvel at an 18-passenger Boeing transport, on public display for the first time, at General Aircraft Company's "flying freight car," which the manufacturer claimed could carry 2,000 pounds of cargo at 135 miles per hour, at the recently developed Ford and Fokker three-engined ships, and at 200,000 sprawling square feet of exhibits offered by every conceivable aviation-related business.

The center of racing activity was 12 miles away at the newly renovated Cleveland Airport. One side of the 1,100-acre field was reserved for commercial operations, including displays of aircraft, accommodations for the hundreds of planes bringing spectators to the races, and the arrivals and departures that constituted the usual business of the airport. Strollers among the commercial hangars could get a close-up look at the latest designs of commercial, private and racing aircraft. From there it was a long, dusty walk past a line of operations buildings and concession stands to the airport's racing section. There, amid the vast grandstands with seating for 50,000 people, stood a five-story administration building with balconies for special guests and the working headquarters of the tireless, imaginative and persuasive promoter who had put the whole show together—Clifford W. "Cliff" Henderson.

The man who had made the National Air Races the biggest, most varied and best attended of aviation's carnivals had begged flying lessons from Army pilots while he was serving as a general's chauffeur in France during World War I. On his return to the United States, he bought three war-surplus Curtiss Jennies and eventually purchased a

Marine Lieutenant Herbert Becker careens his Curtiss F-8 around a pylon manned by judges in a closed-circuit race limited to military aircraft during the 1928 National Air Races in Los Angeles.

hangar at Clover Field in Santa Monica, California—having supplemented his savings by scrounging German helmets, Iron Crosses and similar artifacts from abandoned battlefields after the Armistice and selling them to souvenir-happy soldiers. He swapped one of his Jennies for additional flying lessons, managed eventually to solo, and launched himself in Santa Monica as a Nash automobile dealer by offering a free airplane ride to every buyer.

His salesmanship attracted attention. The Army's round-the-world flying team had gathered for their historic flight of 1924 at Clover Field—near the headquarters of Donald Douglas, who designed the World Cruisers that were used on the flight—before the official start from Seattle. Henderson was asked to provide them with a fitting welcome at Clover Field on their return. When 200,000 people jammed the roads to the field in response to his promotional efforts, he decided that fate was beckoning him toward grander pursuits. He organized a team of stunt fliers known as the Black Falcons, put on a profitable series of weekly flying exhibitions at Clover Field and attracted large crowds in 1928 by staging an International Aeronautical Exposition along with the National Air Races at a barley field that was to become the Los Angeles airport.

It was Henderson's first contact with the nation's foremost aviation event. The annual air races had started in a small way in 1920, using as their example America's first international aviation meet, which had been held in Los Angeles in 1910. In 1922, the National Aeronautic Association was founded and became the sanctioning organization of the races. The early events were known primarily for the Pulitzer Trophy race until that contest was discontinued in 1925. By that time, the federal government's interest in developing high-speed pursuit planes was reflected in the total domination of the races by military aircraft and pilots.

After his success at Los Angeles in 1928, Henderson and his brother Phillip were asked to manage the 1929 races in Cleveland. Henderson was determined to create a marketplace for aviation as well as a prestigious event with national appeal. "Our project is designed as a constructive merchandising medium," he insisted. "The entertainment features are purely incidental."

He nevertheless began planning innovations for the 1929 races, "some of them so daring as to be radical." A women's air race from Santa Monica to Cleveland would give appropriate recognition to the growing number of female pilots. Gliders and lighter-than-air craft would have a place on the program for the first time. An autogyro—an aircraft that used a free-wheeling rotor instead of fixed wings to supply the lift for near-vertical takeoffs and landings—would appear. And Henderson demonstrated his gift for showmanship by introducing the "racehorse" start. Planes had taken off one by one to make timed circuits of earlier courses, but at Cleveland they lined up 50 feet apart before the grandstands, took off together and flew to a special scat-

Managing Director Clifford Henderson cuts a figure as sporty as his Cord convertible at the 1936 National Air Races in Cleveland. The grandstands behind him—almost half a mile long and packed with spectators —testify to his promotional skills.

tering pylon before returning to the triangular pattern they followed for the rest of the race.

Cliff Henderson presided over an army of 8,300 paid staff members and volunteers organized into 49 departments; his brother managed the business side. Their tightly orchestrated masterpiece of organizational and promotional skill cemented Henderson's hold on the races, his status symbolized by a large white touring car parked in front of the carpeted, palm-decked entrance to the race headquarters in the grandstand area.

The schedule called for all commercial demonstration flights to stop at noon and the racing program to begin. Entertainment may have been incidental to Henderson, but for 10 days he never allowed his audiences a dull moment. There were 35 races over the closed course, flown by every conceivable type of aircraft, and cross-country races from points all over the United States, terminating on the racing field.

And there was plenty to see between races. Daredevils of the Army, Navy and Marine Corps, with Charles Lindbergh leading two of the celebrated Navy "High Hats," put on daily demonstrations of tactical maneuvers and aerobatics. A Canadian air force team, flying all-metal Siskin fighters, thoroughly frightened even veteran observers by screaming over the grandstands scant feet above the spectators' heads. Charles "Speed" Holman flew an incredible series of loops, rolls and inverted maneuvers in a three-ton Ford Tri-motor, producing a result that one spectator likened to "an elephant skipping rope." Goodyear blimps and the Navy's metal-clad dirigible (it had a duralumin hull) flew overhead, and the mighty rigid airship U.S.S. *Los Angeles* hooked up with an aircraft in flight high over the crowd. Famous pilots and dignitaries appeared on the grounds, among them Germany's leading airshipman, Hugo Eckener, fresh from his historic circumnavigation of the globe in the *Graf Zeppelin*.

For those who were still able to gaze and gasp after nightfall, there were massive displays of fireworks at the airport and night-flying demonstrations with yet more pyrotechnics over a temporary lakefront airport. Finally, at 11 o'clock each evening there was a musical extravaganza entitled *Wings of Love* conceived by Henderson and boasting a cast of 120 people.

"Nothing like it has ever been seen in America before," enthused one aviation writer, as the 1929 Air Races drew toward a close. But the best was yet to come: the final, closed-course 50-mile free-for-all that would test civilian racing planes against the best pursuit ships the Army and Navy could field.

The planes that threatened military domination of high-speed flight that September were among the first produced by a new generation of intuitive, chronically underfinanced designers and builders—many of them fliers—who operated out of small shops across the country. These grease-stained entrepreneurs were the final flowering of the kind of

Dynamic bursts of ballyhoo

Promoter Cliff Henderson devoted considerable attention to the selection of eye-catching artwork designed to express the spirit of the National Air Races. The 1929 souvenir sticker and the official program covers shown here are from the first five years that Henderson directed the event. All depict the dynamic theme that became the races' instantly recognizable symbol: a checkered pylon with one or more planes whirling hell-for-leather around it. The illustrations for 1931 and 1932 were painted by the renowned aviation artist Charles Hubbell.

Sold by the thousands by grandstand vendors, the colorful programs quickly became collectors' items, cherished mementos of a day at the races.

aviator who assumed, as a matter of course, that individual genius and hard work could compete successfully with professional training, academic credentials and vast resources. Almost all of them had absorbed what they knew of aeronautical science by tinkering with Jennies and Standards as barnstormers and by building, and risking their necks in, later models of their own. They bowed to advancing technology by hiring better-educated men to run stress analyses on their creations, but the basic designs of their racing planes were products of their own shrewd, optimistic and immensely practical minds.

Their era began with the final event of the 1929 National Air Races, and it began because their single-minded, frankly dangerous pursuit of speed had led most of them to abandon the biplane and couple their larger power plants with a single wing in the belief that the monoplane was the aircraft of the future. That view had been encouraged by the successes of the Lockheed Vega at the 1928 Races, where Vegas had placed first in the transcontinental race and both first and second in the civilian free-for-all race.

The Vega, a six-passenger cabin plane faster than any other commercial aircraft, had been designed by a self-educated engineer named John K. Northrop and constructed in a little shop in Hollywood, California, owned by Allan Loughead, who helped to support it, and himself, by working as a real estate agent. Although designed to carry passengers, the plane proved so fast that Frank Hawks used it to set cross-country records in February and June of 1929.

In the climactic free-for-all race at Cleveland, the Vega would be up against another civilian plane, in addition to the military entries. Little was known about the other civilian entry before race time because its builders had kept it shrouded in canvas inside locked hangars almost constantly from its inception. They had been so secretive that the ship had been dubbed the Mystery. It had been designed a year earlier by two young engineers, Herbert Rawdon and Walter Burnham, at Walter Beech's Travel Air Company in Wichita, Kansas. Built to rigid design specifications, it was test-flown in August of 1929 and found to exceed expectations. Its aerodynamic innovations included a new kind of cowling to reduce the turbulence of the airflow over the radial engine and the use of streamlined wheel pants.

The Vega and the Mystery would be competing with the two best pursuit ships the military could muster. Although appropriations for designing and building racing planes had been denied them, both the Army and the Navy had modified their familiar Curtiss Hawks with engine changes and more sophisticated streamlining for the 1929 contest, and conventional wisdom assumed that, once again, the race would be between the two services.

When the starter's flag dropped, the Mystery, flown by Doug Davis of flying-circus fame, immediately forged ahead. But Davis cut inside a pylon and had to turn back to circle it. He fell a mile behind the leading plane, the Army Hawk, but he relentlessly closed the gap, his propel-

The cross-country virtuoso

"Don't telegraph," quipped a 1930s wag, "send it by Hawks." "Hawks" was Iowa-born Frank Hawks, whose specialty was flying against the clock on cross-country routes he selected himself. Sponsored by an oil company, he racked up some 200 city-to-city records by 1931.

Hawks's times were astonishing for the era: London-Paris, 59 minutes; Philadelphia-New York, 20 minutes; Los Angeles-New York, 12 hours 25 minutes. In 1937 Hawks retired from his dangerous career but, ironically, was killed the next year while leisurely flying a Gwinn Aircar, a plane considered so safe and poky it was advertised as everyman's aircraft.

Record-setter Hawks, seen here clad in a fur flying coat, believed that "aviation, to be worth anything, must be fast."

At the Los Angeles mid-point of his cross-country round trip in 1929, Hawks and friends dine at midnight under his plane's wing.

ler singing "like a siren," as one newspaper reported. Walter Beech, a cigar butt clenched between his teeth, paced up and down near the finish line. The Army plane crossed the line first, but since the contestants for this race had started at 10-second intervals it was not until the times were compared that the results were known. The Mystery had won. The Army's Curtiss came in second, the Vega third, and the Navy Hawk fourth.

The military's embarrassment was profound. Their best planes and pilots had been bested by small privately built aircraft. It was a stunning beginning, however, of the age of the back-shop builders and their hot civilian racers. It was apparent that a struggling aircraft builder, like the trainer of a Kentucky Derby winner, could now achieve nationwide recognition overnight; all he had to do was produce a plane capable of leading the pack at the National Air Races.

In 1930, Cliff Henderson applied in Chicago the formula that had been so successful in Cleveland the previous year, with an important addition. He had talked Charles Thompson, a Cleveland manufacturer of automotive and aircraft valves, who had sponsored the free-for-all race of 1929, into offering a new trophy and purse for a closed-course speed race that would be open to any and all aircraft. The trophy was an ornate bronze symbol of the speed fever that had gripped participants and spectators alike during the running of the climactic race of the 1929 program.

The Thompson Trophy race, scheduled for the final day of the 1930 races at Chicago's Curtiss-Reynolds Airport, attracted two designers who were determined to use the Thompson as a springboard to prominence. One of them had just won five closed-course events with a tiny monoplane named *Pete* that he had built in his spare time; the other was still assembling his entry—the *Solution*—at nearby Ashburn Field as race day dawned.

Benjamin Odell "Benny" Howard had made his living during the summer of 1929 by flying passengers and mail in Ford Tri-motor transports between St. Louis and Kansas City for Universal Air Lines. But Howard had larger ambitions, and he pursued them by sitting at home before a full-length mirror, calibrating the cubic dimensions of his body with a yardstick. He wanted to figure out the smallest space in which a pilot could be contained and to build around it a tiny racing plane powered by a little four-cylinder air-cooled engine that would be capable of beating more thunderous machines.

Howard, born poor in Palestine, Texas, in 1904, had gone to work as a roustabout in the Texas oil fields after being forced to leave high school at the age of 16. He went to Dallas in 1923 and got a job as a rigger in a Curtiss plant in which Jennies were reconditioned for sale to the public. He invested $150—$10 down, $10 a month—in a second-hand Standard and soon crashed, killing a passenger and giving himself a permanent limp. "I had read a book on how to fly," he remembered later, "and I didn't think anything more was necessary. I hadn't caught on to some of the very simplest fundamentals. When I got out of the hospital and could hobble around I made a deal with a fellow and he taught me about spinning and all those other things I should have learned before."

Now that he could fly, Howard patched together a biplane—a composite of parts from old Jennies and Standards—and went barnstorming. He met a Houston bootlegger who wanted an airplane that could carry more illegal cargo than the models available. Could Benny adapt a plane to his purposes—and keep his mouth shut? Benny could and did, by deepening the fuselage of a Lincoln Standard and providing high-lift wings. Thus modified, the plane proved capable of transporting 15 full cases of booze at a crack. "Damned good airplane," said his customer, a phrase Howard later abbreviated to DGA and used as a trademark— and as a sardonic commentary on the more pretentious names adopted by other aircraft promoters.

The bootlegger paid him $600 and Howard, soon short of cash again, sold his own biplane for $1,100. Realizing that aviation was changing rapidly, Howard studied navigation and instrument flying, and gained experience with multiengined aircraft. He earned a radio operator's license and, eventually, an air-transport certificate. He discovered that he had become a man of rare skills. "As I remember, there were less than 50 multiengine pilots on the face of the earth," he said. "When they gathered 17 of us together to be checked out on instruments (all we had were turn and rate-of-climb indicators and an altimeter) only two of us got a plane away from the area, let alone got back." He readily found work flying Ford Tri-motors for Universal Air Lines in St. Louis, but he still itched to create his own airplanes.

An institution known as the Von Hoffman Aircraft School stood on Lambert Field at St. Louis and Benny Howard became acquainted with an 18-year-old engineering student there named Gordon Israel. Israel was fascinated by Howard's design ideas and began working on technical drawings for him. Soon they had talked the school into providing them working space in a hangar, and advanced engineering students were doing the mathematical calculations necessary in so sophisticated a design, while Israel superintended construction. DGA 3 was completed—at a cost of $2,500—in July of 1930. It was so tiny that Howard claimed he could not get into the cockpit if he was wearing heavy socks or underwear, but the plane proved easy to fly and to have an amazing top speed of almost 200 miles per hour. Howard painted the name *Pete*—which he somehow felt matched the plane's personality—on its snow-white fuselage and arranged for a pilot to fly it for him at the National Air Races.

Howard's pilot failed to show up in the hours before the start of the meet—a problem he solved with great misgivings by taking the controls himself. He was better prepared for the anarchy of closed-course competition than he thought and was confident enough, after defeating

plane after plane of superior horsepower, to enter the Thompson Trophy race on Labor Day.

Emil M. "Matty" Laird had an entry in the Thompson, too, and like Howard he had a last-minute problem. His pilot showed up—but his plane was not finished. Laird had begun designing model aircraft while he was a youngster in Chicago and had built his first full-sized airplane—it had a 12-horsepower engine—in 1913 while he was working as an office boy at the First National Bank. He rebuilt the plane and improved his performance at the controls during the following year, and in 1915 at the age of 19—having earned the astounding sum of $400 by making two exhibition flights at Sebring, Ohio—he found himself being heralded as a sensation while demonstrating his Laird Baby Biplane at county fairs in Indiana, Kansas, Iowa and Ohio. He built a bigger model, which he called *Boneshaker,* the next year, became the sixth American to fly the inside loop, and invaded South Dakota, Texas, Colorado and Montana. On election night in 1916 he circled above St. Paul, Minnesota, bearing colored lights that signaled readers of the *St. Paul Dispatch*—which had hired Laird and publicized the signal system—whether Woodrow Wilson or Charles Evans Hughes was leading in the presidential election.

Operating as the Laird Aviation Company, he sold plans and instructions by mail to would-be aviators who wanted to build Baby Biplanes. Unlike most stunt fliers, he had a feel for business and organization. After he was lamed in the crash of a plane he was testing in Texas in 1917, he formed the E. M. Laird Airplane Company in Chicago in December 1919. His three-passenger Laird Swallows were considered by many to be the first true commercial aircraft built after World War I, and his line of Laird Speedwings ("Thoroughbreds of the Airways") were among the most respected of small American passenger planes during the following decade. The B. F. Goodrich Company, attracted to the glamor of racing, came to his factory in 1930 to order a custom-built Thompson Trophy contender.

Few incidents better dramatize the casual, can-do attitudes of the era: Neither Laird nor his engineer, R. L. Henrich, was dismayed by the fact that the race was but four weeks away. Nor was Goodrich's pilot, Speed Holman, disturbed by the fact that the Laird *Solution* was not completed and had never been off the ground until one hour before he was due at the starting line at Curtiss-Reynolds Airport on the other side of town.

Holman was accustomed to dealing with such imponderables. For years he had been a parachutist and stunt flier who was particularly celebrated for his improbable aerobatics in a Ford Tri-motor the previous year at the Cleveland races. He stood by patiently as Pratt & Whitney mechanics finished installation of the borrowed 300-horsepower Wasp Jr. radial engine, then climbed into the cockpit, took off for a 10-minute flight, landed, asked for a few minor adjustments, took off again and got the plane to the scene of the race with only minutes to spare.

Emil M. "Matty" Laird points out to Jimmy Doolittle some modifications that have been made on Laird's Super Solution biplane in 1931. Doolittle flew the Super Solution, with its powerful Wasp Jr. radial engine, to victory in the first Bendix transcontinental race that September.

Laird's *Solution* and Howard's *Pete* faced formidable opposition among the seven starters: two Travel Air racers, which were similar to the *Mystery* that had made aviation history the year before, flown by veteran pilots Jimmy Haizlip and Frank Hawks, and a five-year-old Marine Corps Curtiss Hawk flown by Captain Arthur Page, who was intent on salvaging the reputation of military aircraft.

In the race, Captain Page and his much-revised Hawk led the field for 17 of the 20 laps; then disaster struck him. For reasons that were never adequately explained, the Hawk rolled into the ground, fatally injuring Page; it was presumed that he had been poisoned by carbon monoxide. Holman brought the *Solution* in first with an average speed of just over 200 miles per hour, Haizlip was second in a Travel Air, and Howard's little *Pete* took third place.

Matty Laird must be regarded as an anomaly; for while his *Solution* is on the record books forever as the first airplane to win the Thompson Trophy, and while Jimmy Doolittle won the first Bendix Trophy race the following year in a modified version called the *Super Solution,* both the designer and his planes had been outmoded, in the technical sense, even before he built them. Both of the aircraft were biplanes—the last of their type ever to win a major race. Even so, not every replacement for the traditional biplane racer was necessarily an improvement.

Any pilot traveling at more than 200 miles per hour at altitudes under 500 feet was in mortal danger in almost any instance of structural failure or engine malfunction. But no racing plane of the era subjected its pilots to such jeopardy as did the barrel-shaped, lightning-fast and hideously unstable Gee Bees, built by the five Granville brothers of New England—and none lingered so malevolently in American legend after taking the spotlight at the 1931 National Air Races, which were held once again in Cleveland.

New Hampshire-born Zantford D. "Granny" Granville had been attracted to aviation in the early 1920s. He had left school after the eighth grade to become a mechanic, and at the age of 19 established a little automobile-repair garage at Arlington, Massachusetts. He exchanged spare-time work on engines for flying lessons at East Boston Airport, earned a pilot's license in 1925 and soon hit upon a novel means of selling his services to other fliers. He built a portable machine shop on a big truck chassis and with his brothers, Thomas, Robert, Mark and Edward, launched a repair service he called Granville Brothers Aircraft.

Zantford soon designed a little biplane of his own—he set down the design on brown wrapping paper—and his brothers put it together for him in two months. He got it into the air in May 1929 and found that it flew nicely. It had an upper wing that could be adjusted to make possible slow landings and it could be equipped with skis for use on New England snow. When another, wealthier set of brothers—Harry, Frank, George and James Tait of Springfield, Massachusetts—agreed to furnish financial backing, the Granvilles moved to their benefactors' hometown and set up a factory in a defunct dance hall.

The plane sold well for a while, but the company was soon in trouble when the Depression dried up the market for small private planes. The firm's chief engineer, Bob Hall, suggested a daring means of recovery in 1931: a racing plane that could bring home cash prizes. The Granvilles and the Taits created an organization called the Springfield Air Racing Association, and Bob Hall raised money for the payroll by selling shares—including $500 worth bought by a racing pilot named Lowell Bayles. The Granville brothers, working from sketches that Hall produced in feverish progression, hurled themselves into constructing Model Z—later christened *City of Springfield*—the first of the high-powered brutes that were to startle the world of aviation.

Zantford Granville and his colleagues strove for speed by shortening the bulky fuselage, clipping the wings and adding power. But their single-minded passion for high velocity induced suicidal tendencies in the resultant projectile, as racing pilot Jimmy Haizlip discovered one day during his first and only flights in a Gee Bee:

"My first shock came when I touched the rudder. The thing tried to bite its own tail. The next shock I got was when I pulled it around. I got it over past a 30-degree bank and suddenly the stick started coming back at me. She tried to bite herself in the backside again. I landed lovely, except that she stalled at 110 miles per hour."

The stall was an imperfectly understood problem that taunted the designers and endangered the pilots of early airplanes. A wing produces the lift that keeps an aircraft aloft only so long as the flow of air over its surfaces is smooth. If the angle of attack, the relationship of the wing to the flow of air, becomes too great or if the speed of the wing becomes too low, the airflow becomes turbulent and the aircraft stalls, or drops suddenly.

As Jimmy Haizlip discovered, excessively high stall speed was only one of the Gee Bee's problems. "I was feeling quite at home until the third landing," he continued. "I slipped over the trees at 110 miles per hour. Just when I was expecting those wheels to touch, something snapped the left wing down into the ground. The wing broke off with a crash. Both wheels broke off, the right wing broke off, and I went end over end. When I stopped rolling I got out through the little escape hatch. I didn't stop running for about one hundred feet."

Lowell Bayles won the 1931 Thompson Trophy and $7,500 in his Gee Bee in September, flying five of his 10-mile laps at speeds above 240 miles an hour. The Board of Aldermen, the City Council and 6,000 citizens of Springfield turned out to welcome the heroes home and to applaud them as they were paraded through downtown streets. The stockholders, enjoying a 500-per-cent increase in the value of their investment, were more congratulatory yet. But the tragic tale of the Gee Bees had hardly begun. Model Z went out of control during a speed run at Detroit in December, smashed itself to pieces across a half mile of

Ankle-deep in snow, Edward Granville, his brother Zantford and Bob Hall (left to right) display a Gee-Bee Sportster Model E racer outside their workshop, an old dance pavilion, in Springfield, Massachusetts, in 1930. The Model E had a 110-hp Warner Scarab radial engine, and streamlined wheel pants to reduce drag.

railroad track and left Lowell Bayles dead near its flaming wreckage. Bob Hall found opportunities elsewhere and quit the firm. And the pair of thick-bodied Super Sportsters the Granvilles produced thereafter—decorated with painted dice and numbered in honor of the crap-shooters' dream throw, one 7, the other 11—were among the most dangerous airplanes ever flown.

Jimmy Doolittle won the Thompson Trophy with one of the "Bumblebees," the R-1, in 1932, but both the Gee Bees came to grief in 1933. One of them rolled to the left on takeoff at Indianapolis and crashed upside down on the runway. The pilot, Russell Boardman, died as a result of his injuries a few days later. The second plane broke a landing-gear strut after landing at the same airport on the same day in the same race—and, having been repaired, rolled a wing into the ground on landing at Springfield that autumn in the crash that scared the wits out of Jimmy Haizlip and taught him the shortcomings of the airplane's design. Zantford Granville was killed in one of his earlier model sports planes in 1934, as he desperately tried to avoid hitting two construction workers who appeared on a runway at Spartanburg, South Carolina, while he was landing. The pieces of the two original Gee Bee Super Sportsters were salvaged and converted into a third. This hybrid—sponsored by an organization called the Religious Patrons Association and renamed *Spirit of Right*—crashed just after take-off in the Bendix of 1935 and killed yet another pilot.

After 1931, the Bendix Trophy took its place alongside the Thompson as one of the most coveted symbols of the National Air Races. Donated by industrialist Vincent Bendix, manufacturer of starters, electrical devices and brake systems for automobiles and aircraft, the Bendix

Trophy was offered to provide the kind of stimulus to cross-country racing that the Thompson had provided for closed-course speed trials. Jimmy Doolittle won the first Bendix in the Laird *Super Solution,* but for the next three years the coveted trophy was to be presented to pilots seated in James Wedell's monoplanes.

Jimmy Wedell's mother died during his infancy; as a youth he was left to roam in Texas City, Texas, where his father was a waterfront bartender. He discovered, at the age of 11, that he could cadge rides at an Army training field by providing cadets with bottles of whiskey stolen from his father. Later, he got a job in an automobile repair shop that occasionally worked on aircraft engines. Before long he had saved enough money to buy two wrecked planes. He combined them into one that would fly and talked an itinerant pilot into teaching him to fly it. For several years thereafter he wandered around the South as an exhibition flier—the "Air Hobo" from Texas—and as a sometime gunrunner across the Mexican border.

Blind in one eye from a motorcycle accident, Wedell was rejected when he applied for flight training with the Army during World War I. He continued his career as a stunt flier, and while barnstorming in Louisiana in 1927, he met a million-dollar opportunity when he took up a passenger named Harry Williams, a timber tycoon with a thirst for speed. Williams liked his ride so much he bought Wedell's plane, and while learning to fly it he found he liked Wedell, too. They formed a partnership, bought more planes and launched an airline service, with Jimmy and his brother Walter among the pilots, between New Orleans and Houston. And Williams not only approved but furnished unstinted financing when Jimmy began using a corner of a company hangar to build experimental aircraft.

Wedell built his first racer, or at least so legend has it, by drawing an outline in chalk on the hangar floor and then telling mechanics what to place inside it. Wedell was "a real genius," said his shop foreman, Eddie Robertson. "Any man who could take steel tubing, wood, glue and linen and build the world's fastest airplane just out of his head . . . I can't understand to this day how he did it. He said to me, 'Eddie I have too much surface there,' took a piece of yellow crayon and marked off how much smaller he thought it ought to be."

When the plane was finished Wedell expressed his hopes for its future by comparing it with the famed .44-caliber six-gun of the Old West; painted on its fuselage was the legend: "Hot as a 44 and twice as fast." With this plane, thereafter known as the Model 44, Wedell hoped to make a personal sweep of both the Thompson and Bendix races. He never managed that, although he won the Thompson Trophy in 1933. One reason he kept being defeated was that other racing pilots, among them Roscoe Turner, Jimmy Haizlip, Doug Davis and Lee Gehlbach, kept buying and flying Jimmy Wedell's monoplanes too. No other airplane so dominated the National Air Races. Wedell-Williams mono-

The Gee Bee's fateful sting

In the 1920s, Lowell R. Bayles, a shy, soft-spoken barnstormer, was badly bitten by the speed bug. The bug appeared to him in the form of one of the Gee Bees built by the Granville brothers of Springfield, Massachusetts, and—as in the cases of several others who flew those wickedly fast racers—the consequences were calamitous.

Bayles traded in his trusty Jenny for a Gee Bee Model X, and eventually, wanting an even faster plane, switched to another of the temperamental, quirky Granville speed machines, the Model Z. Piloting it barefooted (for better control, he said), he went after the world landplane speed record held since 1924 by Florentin Bonnet: 278 mph.

In December of 1931 in Detroit, Bayles reached 281.9 mph in his Model Z, but he was denied the record because rules stipulated that the new time had to better the old record by at least 4.73 mph to be official. Four days later he tried again. Diving from an altitude of 1,000 feet, he was clocked at over 300 mph as he flashed along the 3-kilometer (1.86-mile) course just 75 feet off the ground. The time would never be official, because the Gee Bee then pitched up sharply, a wing buckled and the plane spun twice and arced into the earth (following pages).

Lowell Bayles helps his mechanic fasten the canopy on his Granville Gee Bee before his try at the world speed record.

Bayles's Gee Bee (left) streaks over the speed course at Detroit's Wayne County Airport. A few moments later Bayles apparently lost control when a gas cap worked itself loose and smashed through the windshield into his face. The plane crashed, producing a violent explosion (above). Bayles was killed instantly.

planes placed 1-2-3 in the Bendix race of 1932, 1-2 in 1933, 1-2 in 1934 and second in 1935. Their record in the Thompson was similar: second in 1931, 2-3-4 in 1932, 1-2 in 1933 and 1-3 in 1934.

Misfortune brought a sudden end to this dazzling string of successes in 1934. A tropical hurricane hit Patterson, Louisiana, in June and in minutes turned all but one of Harry Williams' fleet of aircraft into junk. Williams decided to sell the surviving plane, a Gypsy Moth, and when an interested bidder came along, Jimmy Wedell took him up to teach him to fly. Apparently the student grabbed the stick and froze in fear; the plane suddenly nosed up, stalled, fell out of control and crashed. The student survived with slight injuries, but Wedell was dead when his brother Walter reached the wreckage. Walter himself died in a crash the following summer, and Harry Williams was killed a year after that when a Beechcraft in which he was a passenger lost power on takeoff at Baton Rouge and disintegrated in a nearby grove.

Designers Gordon Israel (left) and Benjamin Howard inspect the Pratt & Whitney Wasp SE engine that powered their 1935 Bendix Trophy entry, Mister Mulligan. Built to comply with safety regulations for commercial aircraft, the high-winged monoplane could carry four passengers in its fully enclosed cabin.

Benny Howard—he of the Damned Good Airplanes—made fewer headlines than Wedell and the Granvilles as they wrote their chapters in aviation history, but he widened his base in racing nevertheless and took home a good deal more prize money than many of his peers. He built two more tiny planes—one named *Mike* and the other *Ike*—after bringing *Pete* home third in the Thompson Trophy race of 1930, and his trio of little white monoplanes proved almost as successful in limited competition as did Jimmy Wedell's monoplanes in races for more powerful aircraft. Both new planes were equipped with Menasco engines that gave them speeds considerably in excess of 200 miles per hour, and in 1933 *Mike*—flown by a pilot named Roy Minor—managed a third in the Thompson.

Racing remained a sideline for Howard as he continued to fly passenger planes as a captain for United Air Lines. However, United's president, William A. Patterson, decided that his company's captains had no business in the cockpits of racing aircraft, and Howard's speedy little monoplanes were flown by other pilots thereafter, particularly by Minor and another veteran of closed-circuit competition named Harold Neumann.

But none of this interfered with Howard's lifelong preoccupation with design. He nursed the idea that he might be able to design a family air sedan with speed enough, despite its unromantic outlines, to win the Bendix Trophy. Thus was conceived DGA 6—better known as *Mister Mulligan.*

This revolutionary plane—put together in four months in 1934 at an abandoned aircraft plant at Kansas City—was built around the kind of big radial engine that had become the standard source of speed in racing planes: a $5,500 Pratt & Whitney 500-horsepower Wasp SE (which was modified to deliver up to 830 horsepower for racing). The plane was also equipped with a controllable pitch propeller, a device that was just coming into general use. Howard had not only seized upon all available power but, in search of extra speed, had designed his bulky creation to fly in thin air at high altitude. His daring hopes were realized when he took the plane to 17,000 feet on a test flight and found himself cruising at 290 miles per hour while using just 75 per cent of his power.

He chose Harold Neumann and an airline pilot named George Cassidy to fly *Mister Mulligan* in the Bendix race. He told them to fly at 17,000 feet on their trip from Kansas City to Burbank, California, where the coast-to-coast Bendix contest was to begin, and when they asked if they would need to use the oxygen they carried on board, Howard assured them that he had encountered no problems at all in flying the plane at that altitude.

Neumann and Cassidy did as they were instructed and noticed nothing unusual until they had passed over Denver—perhaps because a person who is being gradually deprived of oxygen, like one who is being gradually oversupplied with alcohol, often experiences an unwarranted cheerfulness of outlook. Neumann was not aware that notes he was making in the log were becoming increasingly illegible, but he did finally notice, after hauling the ship up to 21,000 feet to avoid a barrier of high clouds, that Cassidy seemed to have fallen asleep and had turned "kind of blue." Neumann began to feel cold and apprehensive, and when the engine stopped he was unable to imagine what had happened to it. He puzzled groggily over this development as *Mister Mulligan* headed for the earth below.

Neumann managed to maintain control of the plane as it coasted lower, and he eventually revived somewhat as he found himself in a ravine below the level of the mountaintops. He had been fumbling with fuel valves and finally managed to tap the main tank and restart the engine. Now he was lost. At the outset of the flight, having failed to locate a set of aeronautical charts bearing radio frequencies, he had blithely set forth with a handful of tourist maps. He found a railroad line, followed it, spotted a distant airstrip and prepared in befuddled gratitude to land. He almost made it; but a crosswind hit *Mister Mulligan* as the wheels touched, and the plane careened into a ridge left by grading machines and wiped out both the landing gear and propeller before coming to rest.

And there, near Hawthorne, Nevada, *Mister Mulligan* reposed as Doug Davis won the Bendix race of 1934 in one of Jimmy Wedell's racers. Engineer Gordon Israel (who had rejoined Howard to help build the ship) found it necessary to dismantle *Mister Mulligan,* haul the pieces over 350 miles of mountain roads and make repairs in Los Angeles. Howard found himself $17,500 in the hole by the time his creation was returned to operation. He approached United's President Patterson with an eloquent tale of hard luck in the hope of getting permission to try to win some of it back in the Bendix race of 1935. Patterson finally agreed. Closed-circuit racing was out, but the Bendix . . . well . . . all right.

Acutely aware that the hard-charging Roscoe Turner would be right behind him, Howard started the race in a thick fog at Burbank with Gordon Israel as his copilot. They climbed to 17,000 feet and sucked frequently on rubber tubes that protruded from a bottle of oxygen. Thus fortified, they stayed at their great height until they approached Kansas City, where they landed and refueled. Returning quickly to altitude, they cruised into Cleveland, defeating Roscoe Turner by a margin of 23.5 seconds.

Only much later did Howard confess, with a certain red-faced pride, that his plane had raced under a handicap after leaving Kansas City. "When we were in the neighborhood of Toledo I thought I'd tune in on the Detroit range, but when I started to turn on the radio I had trouble reaching it. I had a big bar for pulling down the flaps; it was in the way and I'd never had that trouble before. Finally it dawned on me. We had flown from Kansas City with the flaps down! I was so embarrassed that I didn't tell anybody. But then I got to thinking, why am I keeping

A waving flag welcomes Frank Fuller to Teterboro, New Jersey, in 1937. Fuller had won the Los Angeles-to-Cleveland Bendix Trophy race and kept going to set a transcontinental speed record of 9 hours 35 minutes. The Seversky he flew was a modified Army P-35 fighter.

this a secret? After all, I beat Roscoe Turner with my flaps down.''

As euphoric as though *Mister Mulligan* had won by an hour, Howard was even happier when Harold Neumann agreed to fly *Mister Mulligan*—despite the restrictions on visibility imposed by its enclosed cabin—in the Thompson Trophy race as well. Roscoe Turner's Wedell-Williams seemed unbeatable in the Thompson, until his engine blew up on the ninth of ten 15-mile laps, and *Mister Mulligan* crossed the finish line first again—winning $6,750 to add to the $4,500 already won with the Bendix Trophy. Big and ungainly it may have been, but *Mister Mulligan* was the only airplane ever to win both the Thompson and the Bendix Trophies in the same year.

Streamlined beauties that set the pace

"It is useless to hope to attain higher speeds by power alone," wrote a racing-plane designer in 1929. "We must clean up parasite resistance." The designers did just that in creating the elegant aircraft shown on these and the following pages—machines in which form was responsive to function to an almost unprecedented degree.

As early as 1925, racing-plane engines were producing a full horsepower for each pound of their own weight, a ratio rarely exceeded until the advent of jet propulsion.

Designers wrestled with the problem of how to get more speed from their planes without increasing engine weight. They gradually abandoned the biplane for the monoplane, wood for light metals, and traditionally heavy engines for lightweight monobloc engines. By trial and sometimes fatal error they learned how to streamline radiators, to improve shock-absorbing systems and eventually to retract the landing gear. In the end they created the swiftest vehicles the world had ever known.

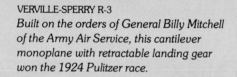

VERVILLE-SPERRY R-3
Built on the orders of General Billy Mitchell of the Army Air Service, this cantilever monoplane with retractable landing gear won the 1924 Pulitzer race.

CURTISS R3C-2
Equally successful as a landplane and a seaplane, the R3C-2 could climb 5,000 feet in a minute. It was the last biplane to win the Schneider race (1925).

MACCHI M.39
This all-wood 1926 Schneider winner, designed by Mario Castoldi of Italy, was an aerodynamic masterpiece that became a model for seaplane racers.

TRAVEL AIR MODEL R "MYSTERY SHIP"
By beating military racers in the 1929 Thompson race, the Model R popularized low-winged monoplanes and opened the way for civilian designers.

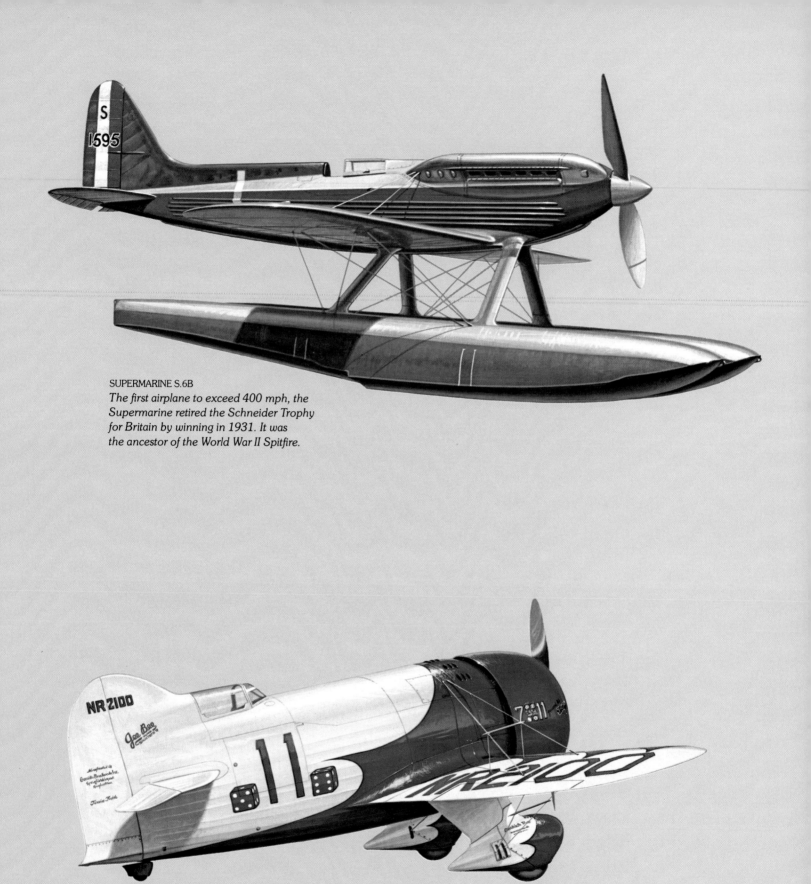

SUPERMARINE S.6B
The first airplane to exceed 400 mph, the Supermarine retired the Schneider Trophy for Britain by winning in 1931. It was the ancestor of the World War II Spitfire.

GEE BEE R-1
Built to house the huge Pratt & Whitney Wasp Jr. engine, this most famous of American racers won the 1932 Thompson but was notoriously hard to handle.

WEDELL-WILLIAMS 44
On markedly thin wings, the spruce-and-welded-steel 44 won more races (including the 1933 Thompson and 1934 Bendix) than any other plane of its day.

HOWARD MISTER MULLIGAN
Winner of both the Thompson and Bendix Trophies in 1935, this enclosed monoplane was the only racer to evolve successfully into a commercial plane.

CAUDRON C-460
Equipped with wing flaps, retractable landing gear and a variable pitch propeller, the revolutionary French-built Caudron won the Thompson race in 1936.

FOLKERTS SK-3 JUPITER
The 1937 Thompson winner exemplified American trial-and-error design. It had a wooden propeller of very high pitch and one of the shortest wingspans in racing.

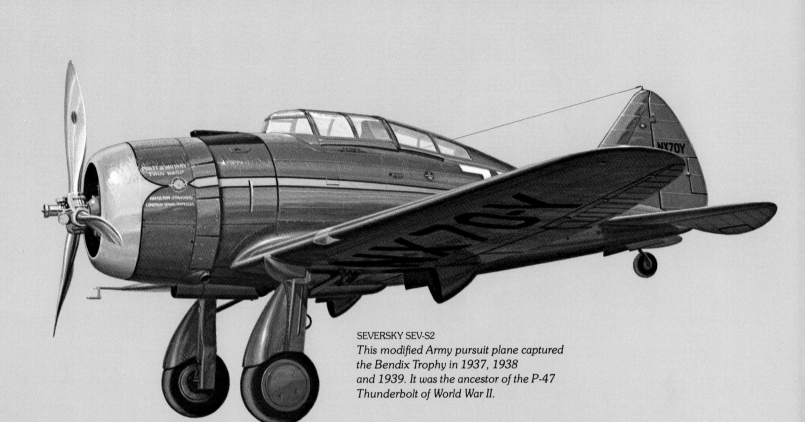

SEVERSKY SEV-S2
This modified Army pursuit plane captured
the Bendix Trophy in 1937, 1938
and 1939. It was the ancestor of the P-47
Thunderbolt of World War II.

LAIRD-TURNER LTR-14
The high-powered LTR had a unique
wooden fuselage covered half in metal and
half in fabric. Nicknamed Miss Champion, it
won the 1938 and 1939 Thompson.

Recordsetters that never raced

Two of the greatest racers of the 1930s never participated in a race. Italian designer Mario Castoldi's masterful seaplane, the M.C. 72 *(right)*, set its remarkable 440-mph speed record in 1933—two years after the Schneider seaplane contests were over. Howard Hughes's revolutionary H-1 Special *(above)* set a land speed record of 352.38 mph in 1935. Hughes intended to enter the airplane in the 1936 Thompson race but decided against it and went on to prepare for a more spectacular achievement: In 1937 he piloted the H-1 on a record-breaking transcontinental flight of 7 hours 28 minutes.

Efforts to interest the United States Army in the H-1 as a pursuit plane failed, partly because it was not built to standard Army specifications. In 1937, after having flown some 40 hours, the plane was retired to a humidity-controlled hangar of the Hughes Aircraft Company in California, never to fly again.

MACCHI-CASTOLDI M.C. 72
Equipped with contrarotating propellers to eliminate torque and almost covered with radiators to dissipate heat, the brilliantly streamlined M.C. 72 flew 100 mph faster than the best landplanes of its time.

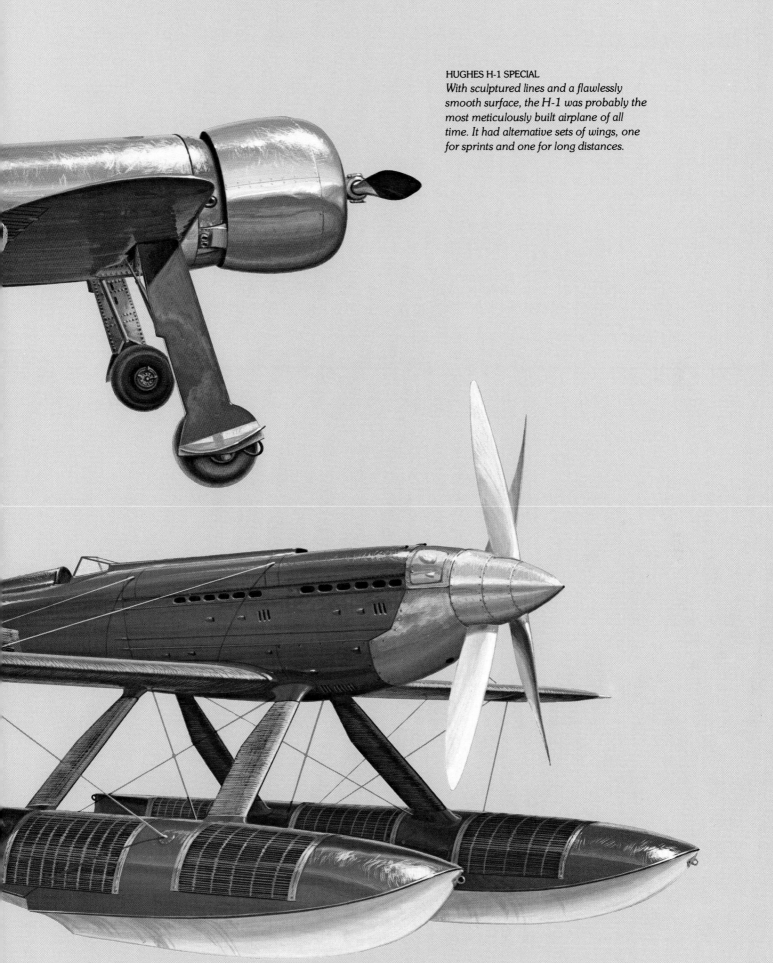

HUGHES H-1 SPECIAL
With sculptured lines and a flawlessly smooth surface, the H-1 was probably the most meticulously built airplane of all time. It had alternative sets of wings, one for sprints and one for long distances.

139

Theater in the sky

During the 1930s, the National Air Races at Cleveland sometimes seemed to belong to the Labor Day weekend as fireworks belonged to the Fourth of July. "People would save their pennies and dimes," said racing pilot Harold Neumann, "and come from all over the country riding their motorcycles, bicycles and cars to take their vacation at the Cleveland air races." As many as 100,000 ticket holders jammed the grounds and the grandstand; thousands more watched the low-flying racers from nearby rooftops, trees, fences and even telephone poles.

Impresario Cliff Henderson's crowd-pleasing technique was to keep something happening before the stands every moment from noon until late at night. A typical day began with qualifying speed trials, proceeded to a midday opening fanfare by the Texaco Fire Chief Band, and continued with a mixture of stunt flying, comedy acts and simulated dogfights and bombings designed to hold the crowd during intervals between the speed contests that gave the extravaganza its name.

Some young men and women who had come to the races intending merely to gawk stayed to enlist in the mass parachute jump; they were paid as little as $10 to risk their necks leaping from a plane. Other acts became instant classics, such as Mike Murphy's amazing feat of landing on and taking off from a platform atop a moving automobile, and the Army's snakelike snap-the-whip formation of pursuit planes looping on one another's tails. At night there were more acrobatics, and planes that fired rockets from their wing tips.

In the races themselves, which started at a home pylon in front of the stands, the pilots flew as low as they dared, skimming just over the tops of the houses, high-tension lines and trees that dotted the flat Ohio landscape. Part of the appeal of both races and acrobatics was the highly evident danger involved—a factor that led to increasing criticism in the press ("A Roman holiday," observed the *New York Times*). Considering the risks, the event's safety record was not all that bad. But those who came hoping to see the specter of death at work were not always disappointed: Nine pilots were killed in a decade of the show.

United States Boeing P-12 fighters, flying in a stepped V formation, pass low over the National Air Races crowd at Cleveland in 1931. The grandstand, the largest ever built for an air show, had a capacity of 50,000.

Parachutists land near a ceremonial cannon at Cleveland in 1932. Jumping from 5,000 feet, the chutists aimed to land on a

painted bull's-eye, but sometimes they missed the 1,000-acre field altogether.

Racers take off in front of the stands at the beginning of a 100-mile dash during the 1936 National Air Races in Los Angeles. Harold Neumann, flying

a Folkerts Special named Toots (center), won this contest with an average speed of 223 miles per hour.

Split seconds of drama are captured in this newsreel sequence from the 1936 races in Los Angeles. Reading from left to right, the undercarriage of Joe Jacobson's monoplane, Mike, collapses as he comes in for a landing, and the plane noses over and cartwheels. Jacobson was unhurt.

5

A winning pair of kings

Only one man was paying attention at first as a powerful Curtiss Hawk was prepared for takeoff at Dayton, Ohio's, Wright Field on the morning of May 25, 1927. "Watch the sky over there," the pilot had told him, "and tell me what you see." That was tip-off enough. The word that something was up spread quickly among mechanics and aviators as a slight, handsome lieutenant named James H. Doolittle climbed into the pursuit ship, and by the time he took off, a small, intent crowd had gathered. Jimmy Doolittle was 30 years old and was already famous for his exploits in the air—and occasionally on the ground. Glowing newspaper accounts had burnished his reputation as a test pilot without fear who would try absolutely anything in an airplane. Few except his fellow aviators knew that his stunts usually had a specific purpose related to the advancement of aeronautics.

Doolittle had spent six months preparing for this day, mostly poring over aerodynamic calculations. He then tested the calculations in weeks of practice in the Curtiss Hawk, flying strange maneuvers, and returning to Wright Field each night to record and analyze his observations.

He knew, as he reached 10,000 feet and leveled off on this fine spring morning, that he was about to exert an extraordinary force on his aircraft and himself. His plane was stressed to take it, so he expected that the airframe would hold up. But neither he nor any physician he had consulted knew what would happen to the human body when subjected to such stress in the way he proposed to apply it.

Doolittle pointed the nose of the Curtiss Hawk straight down and watched the air-speed indicator climb toward the aircraft's maximum. He then pushed his stick forward and, at 350 miles per hour, began flying an outside loop, his feet toward the center of the circle.

At the bottom of the loop, where the stress was greatest, his vision turned red from the blood rushing down to his head. His body strained the safety harness with 450 pounds of force. Still he kept the stick forward, as the craft slowed, reaching upside down for the sky.

At the moment Doolittle knew he could take no more, when he felt he must pull out, he saw the horizon again. He had completed the loop. Those watching on the ground jubilantly confirmed that Jimmy Doolittle had once more done the impossible.

Reporters soon converged on him to learn the details of his latest feat, and the jaunty pilot told them what he thought they expected to hear. Why had he risked such fearsome odds merely to do an aerobatic trick?

Trailing parallel plumes of smoke, a trio of fliers performs loops at a 1938 air show. The technique of using chemical smoke as a means of making aerial patterns visible was patented by English aeronautical engineer J. C. Savage, who in 1922 astounded England by writing advertising messages across the sky.

"Just thought of it on the spur of the moment," grinned Doolittle.

Such skill, confidence and courage soon were to bring Jimmy Doolittle to the forefront of a new breed of daredevil fliers: the civilian racing pilots of the 1930s. Chance, eccentricities of design and the added danger of low-level flight made racing the most unpredictable of undertakings, but its challenges and cash prizes attracted dozens of fliers willing to slave for months to wring more speed from their temperamental machines and ready to risk everything to be first across the finish line and claim the Thompson or Bendix Trophy. Doolittle and a big, splendidly flamboyant Southerner named Roscoe Turner would become the most heralded among this reckless band. Speed was their Holy Grail, the flying machines they designed, built or adapted themselves were their mounts and the National Air Races their annual tournament.

To this epic decade Doolittle and Turner brought many similar experiences. Both were in their early twenties when they learned to fly during World War I—Turner qualifying in a Curtiss Jenny just as the War was ending. Both drew attention with a special blend of flying skill and personality. Each was adventurous, with a watchful mind and uncanny reflexes. Each felt a duty to contribute to the advancement of aviation.

Yet for all the two men shared, they were completely different in appearance, temperament and background. Doolittle was small, standing five feet six inches and weighing 130 pounds. Turner seemed larger than life—not only because he stood six feet one inch and weighed 225 pounds, but because of his enormous ebullience and vast appetite for food, drink, speed and the heady sound of applause. Doolittle had mastered the theory of flight and held a doctor of science degree. Turner had completed the 10th grade. Doolittle stayed in the service after the War and was provided with the most advanced aircraft available. Turner turned to barnstorming in a middle-aged Jenny for his living. Doolittle, holder of a transcontinental speed record set in 1922 and winner of the Schneider Trophy race in 1925, was considered the Army's hottest pilot. Turner, born in log-cabin poverty near Corinth, Mississippi, seemed in 1927 an unlikely candidate for national recognition.

In the years after the Armistice, Roscoe Turner and stunt pilot Arthur Starnes scraped up a living by performing at county fairs in the Deep South in their mutually owned Jenny. Turner might have been just one barnstormer among hundreds had it not been for his princely air and his unabashed instinct for self-promotion. The Jenny—despite its divided ownership—flew as The Roscoe Turner Flying Circus, and Turner did his best to project a romantic image to match the exaggeration.

Most barnstormers wore boots and leather jackets to distinguish themselves from lesser mortals, but to Turner, his fellow aviators looked like "a lot of tramps and grease monkeys." Men who did their own repairs and slept under the wings of their planes in hard times might be excused for not being flashy dressers. But beyond that, these men who talked of danger with wry understatement shared a contempt for ostentation. Turner embraced it: He sported a needle-pointed waxed mustache and uniforms he designed for maximum impact on his audiences.

These splendid costumes featured blue tunics, cut to resemble those of British officers, and riding breeches of an indefinable hue called ''pinks'' by military tailors. Accessories included buttons bearing the initials ''RT,'' a polished Sam Browne belt and gleaming cavalry boots. Turner wore a gold-and-crimson helmet in the air, stuffing powder puffs into the ear flaps to deaden sound, and switched to a blue officer's cap on the ground. He displayed on his chest a set of gold-and-platinum wings that grew more ornate with time and were eventually studded— he claimed—with ''four or five thousand dollars worth of diamonds.'' With a bottle of Carbona and a towel handy to take care of oil stains, Turner's dress was, he boasted, ''suitable for all occasions.''

His fellow pilots seem to have accepted these shocking departures from the standards of the clan with reluctant admiration after he remained unaffected, even pleased, by their initial hoots of derision. ''A pilot with nerve enough to wear that uniform,'' commented the *Aero Digest,* ''is bound to come in first eventually.'' Turner agreed. ''Let them razz me all they please,'' he said. ''It's a matter of advertising.''

In 1925 he managed to buy an 18-passenger Sikorsky transport— then one of the largest airplanes in the United States—and with it exercised his flair for publicity in a series of outlandish projects. He toured the country with his aircraft decked out as a flying cigar store, took society women aloft for tea, flew a baby grand piano to Washington, D.C., for Mrs. Calvin Coolidge and in 1928 headed for Hollywood to fly in Howard Hughes's movie *Hell's Angels.* His Sikorsky was crashed by another pilot while it was posing as a German bomber for the movie's final aerial scene, and Turner soon turned to running a Los Angeles-to-Reno air service for a group of businessmen. With Reno's easy divorces in mind, he called one of its Lockheed Vegas ''The Alimony Special.'' He enjoyed Hollywood's social life and introduced a number of movie stars—among them Miriam Hopkins, Carole Lombard, Clark Gable, Loretta Young and Fred MacMurray—to the air.

Turner teetered continuously between ornate solvency and bankruptcy, and he strove, just as continuously, to sustain his expensive way of life. In 1930, his gaudiest inspiration occurred on seeing the picture of a lion on a billboard advertising the Gilmore Oil Company. He was lusting at the time for a new airplane, a Lockheed Air Express that had been flown from Los Angeles to Cleveland in a record 13 hours 15 minutes. He contrived a meeting with Earl B. Gilmore, president of the company. If Gilmore would buy the plane and employ him as pilot, Turner promised to set additional intercity speed records and win acres of front-page space for his sponsor by strapping a live lion—to be named Gilmore—into the copilot's seat on every flight.

Gilmore could not resist. He wrote a check for $15,000 to pay for the airplane and Turner hurried off to the World Jungle Compound, near Ventura, which he had found in the yellow pages—this being the Los

Clasping the paw of his lion cub, Gilmore, Roscoe Turner strikes a pose that brought him instant celebrity. The partnership lasted six months, until Gilmore grew too large to fit into the cockpit.

Angeles telephone book—under the heading Lions. Dismayed to find that a full-grown lion cost $200, Turner talked the owner into donating a five-week-old cub to the greater glory of American aviation. He was immediately entranced with his new pet, mainly because of the attention he received while walking the little monster on a leash.

Few captains of industry have been able to buy the kind of newspaper space Earl Gilmore got for his $15,000. Photographers pursued Turner and his feline companion from the first, especially when, at the outraged insistence of the Los Angeles Humane Society, Gilmore the lion was equipped with his own parachute. Charmed aviation writers reported that the cub enjoyed flying and often snoozed contentedly at Turner's side. Hotels clamored to house the pair free of charge, even though Turner insisted that Gilmore share his luxury suites.

Gilmore created a sensation at the National Air Races of 1930, made stage appearances with Eddie Cantor and Joe E. Brown and enlivened innumerable banquets, at which he sometimes would leave his seat to gnaw on the shoes of guests. Turner began wearing a lion-skin

A wary Roscoe Turner tussles with an exuberantly full-grown Gilmore following the lion's retirement. After the lion's death he was stuffed and mounted and was eventually donated to the National Air and Space Museum in Washington.

greatcoat provided, he liked to say, by one of Gilmore's uncles.

Gilmore grew at an alarming rate, however, and after six months Turner was forced with great reluctance to return him to the Jungle Compound. Man and cat had logged 30,000 air miles in the United States, Canada and Mexico before being separated, and Turner had become so famous from coast to coast that cartoonist Zack Mosley was inspired to depict the freewheeling flier as *Smilin' Jack* in a syndicated comic strip. Turner never forgot his leonine friend and mailed $40 to California every month for the rest of Gilmore's life to buy meat for his meals. "The lion kept me for a long while," he would say, "and now I have to be a good sport and keep him." When Gilmore died at the age of 17, Turner had the beast stuffed and kept it in his trophy room for the rest of his own life. "He's not one of the trophies," Turner would assure visitors. "The trophies belong to him as much as they do to me."

Aside from the publicity, Turner's curious agreement with the Gilmore Oil Company had given him, for the first time, unlimited use of a genuinely fast airplane. He just missed breaking Charles Lindbergh's west-to-east transcontinental record when forced down short of Roosevelt Field on May 13, 1930, but he smashed Frank Hawks's east-to-west mark by a half hour two weeks later and beat Lindbergh's time in a second try. After years of struggling to assert himself in aviation, Turner stood on the brink—by the time the great publicity stunt was over—of a career as one of the most formidable of American racing pilots.

Jimmy Doolittle spent his early boyhood in Nome, Alaska—to which his father, a carpenter with a yen for travel and a dream of striking it rich, had been lured by the gold rush of 1896. It was a tough, lawless town in which children were as tough and lawless as their elders. Jimmy, a small boy cursed with an angelic face and long, curly hair, drew frequent challenges, which he met with a heedless pugnacity. At the age of five he bloodied the nose of an Eskimo boy who tried to bully him. ("He thought he was dying. I thought I had killed an Eskimo. We both ran home to our mothers.") He was soon well known for the wild, head-on fury with which he attacked opponents bigger than he.

His mother took him to Los Angeles in 1908 and entered him in Manual Arts High School. Typically, he was soon brawling. A boxing coach named Forest Bailey warned him, with rueful admiration: "You're going to get hurt badly one of these days. You let your emotions rule your body." Bailey offered to teach him boxing. Doolittle agreed, and rewarded his teacher by becoming amateur bantamweight champion of the Pacific Coast at the age of 15. He was an undergraduate at the University of California in 1917 when the United States entered World War I and promptly signed up for training as an Army aviator. He talked his best girl, Josephine Daniels, into getting married—on total funds of $25—while he was on Christmas leave during preflight training.

Doolittle won his wings in March 1918 and had hopes of seeing combat in France. Instead, he was shipped around the States and, finally, just before the War ended, back to Rockwell Field near San Diego—as an instructor. He used his spare time to master aerobatics, pushing himself and the available Jennies or Thomas Morse S-4C Scouts—single-seater pursuit ships then used in advanced training—ever closer to their limits. He was soon regarded as fearless by admirers who did not realize that his apparent recklessness was a product of the same method and self-discipline he had adopted in boxing.

Doolittle's attitude toward regulations put him in constant conflict with his commanding officer, Colonel Harvey Burwell. During the five months Doolittle served as an instructor at Rockwell Field he cracked up several aircraft, was confined to base for three months and was grounded for six weeks as the increasingly frustrated Burwell tried to bring him to heel. On one memorable day motion-picture director Cecil B. De Mille was granted permission to shoot background scenes at Rockwell Field and, before taking his leave, ran the most "interesting" of the footage as a courtesy to Colonel Burwell. There on the screen was Lieutenant Doolittle; he had been practicing stunts on the wings of a Jenny flown by fellow sinner John McCulloch and now was perched between the plane's wheels and grinning as it came in for a landing. "Ground Doolittle for a month!" shouted Burwell.

Still, it was not long before Doolittle talked Burwell into approving a special mission. A flight from their field to Washington, D.C., Doolittle contended, would demonstrate the Air Service's mastery of navigation and its ability to deliver confidential messages to the seat of government. And so bold an undertaking, he promised, would result in national publicity for Burwell's command.

On a spring morning in 1919 Doolittle led his flight of three Curtiss Jennies into the air to make aviation history. But they got no farther east than Needles, California, some 200 miles away, before the other two aircraft had crashed. Doolittle turned back—and crash-landed himself.

"Doolittle," exploded the colonel, "you're a damned Chinese Ace. Know what that is? That's a pilot who wrecks more of his own country's planes than he does of the enemy's." "Yes, sir," said Doolittle. But he was already planning to try again.

It was more than three years later, on September 4, 1922, that he finally did make aviation history and the first of the banner headlines that were to be the hallmarks of his career. He flew an open cockpit D.H.4 from Pablo Beach, Florida, to San Diego, California—with one stop for fuel at Kelly Field, Texas—in 21 hours 20 minutes, becoming the first to cross the continent in less than a day. After two more years at the Massachusetts Institute of Technology, Lieutenant Doolittle earned one of the first doctorates in aeronautical science granted in the United States. His grasp of advanced aeronautical-engineering theory made him one of the most valuable aviators of his day.

That value was recognized in 1928 when Doolittle was named director of the Full Flight Laboratory, financed by the Guggenheim Fund, at Mitchel Field, New York, to work on improving the safety of flight in

Spectacular showcase in the sun

The sun-blessed coastal city of Miami, Florida, convinced that it possessed "terrain, accessibility and climate" ideally suited to aircraft, inaugurated its municipal airfield in 1929 with the first of a series of shows that for a decade were surpassed only by the National Air Races as a showcase of American aviation.

Operating in the dead of winter when other air shows were grounded, Miami attracted the nation's best stunt pilots and racers as well as a large contingent of military airplanes. Army and Navy units played such an important role, in fact, that the show eventually dropped the word "races" from its title and adopted the more military-sounding Miami All-American Air Maneuvers. Audiences were treated to mock air battles so intricate they required the building of minia-

ture cities and ammunition dumps—and the services of dirigibles, bombers, fighter planes and antiaircraft batteries.

Military pilots destined to become famous in World War II—among them General Claire Chennault of the Flying Tigers—first came to national prominence while performing at Miami. For American plane builders, the show became a useful proving ground for amphibious designs—thanks to a series of races that required precision landings and takeoffs on adjacent Biscayne Bay.

Paradoxically, the event was a victim of its own success. Backers had predicted that the show would help make Miami "a natural aviation center of the United States." It did. After the War, the skies over the city became so congested that the maneuvers were canceled for good.

Banking precariously over watching pilots and ground crews, five civilian racers round a pylon at the Miami air show in 1931.

poor weather. He spent almost a year in dogged experimental flights that pioneered the use of instruments—among them the artificial horizon, the directional gyro, an accurate altimeter and a device that responded visually to radio frequencies to tell the pilot where his aircraft was relative to the transmitting antenna. On September 24, 1929, in a Consolidated NY-2 with a lightproof hood placed over his cockpit, he took off from Mitchel Field and, relying entirely on instruments, flew a carefully calculated rectangular course, landing ("a little sloppily," he said) to complete the first recognized blind flight.

The newspapers trumpeted the accomplishment, *The New York Times* saying on its front page that aviation "had perhaps taken its greatest single step forward in safety." Doolittle, in his usual offhand way, merely remarked that the flight had seemed simple to him, "although we aviators try to make things look difficult."

The end of 1929 brought Doolittle an offer from private industry. Shell Petroleum had set up an aviation department in St. Louis to

Without pausing to undo his parachute, a coolly intent Jimmy Doolittle starts to refuel his Laird Super Solution at Cleveland's Municipal Airport moments after winning the 1931 Bendix. A few minutes later he was racing eastward again on his way to a new speed record from coast to coast.

develop the market for aviation fuels, and wanted Doolittle to publicize the company by entering air races all over the country. Doolittle, still a first lieutenant making only $200 a month as his 33rd birthday approached, resigned from the Air Corps and was given a major's commission in the reserve. On February 15, 1930, he joined Shell, and in an incident reminiscent of his early Army days, he cracked up a brand-new $25,000 Lockheed Vega his first day on the job.

That incident past, he launched his new career by buying the remains of a wrecked Beech Travel Air Mystery and redesigning its fuselage and aileron system while restoring it to airworthiness. The design changes proved disastrous. As Doolittle reached 300 miles per hour—an astonishing speed for the day—on a low-level test run at St. Louis' Curtiss-Steinberg Field, the ailerons began to flutter and the wings began to come apart. He managed to climb to 400 feet, roll the plane on its back and bail out. Seconds later he hit the ground, bruised, breathless but miraculously alive. He seemed less upset by his narrow escape than by the sight of his expensive airplane going up in smoke.

By the summer of 1931 he was in Chicago looking at a possible replacement: an improved version of the Laird *Solution,* the biplane racer in which Charles Holman had won the Thompson Trophy at Chicago in 1930. The new *Super Solution* was full of bugs. The side area of the undercarriage streamlining and engine cowling caught the wind and made the ship difficult to control, especially at high speed. It took off reluctantly because the propeller pitch was set for high-speed operation, and it had to be landed very fast because of its high stalling speed. More serious, its rigging went flabby after a short time in the air and it became impossible to get the plane out of a left bank at cruising speed without throttling back. As a result, pilots tried to make right turns only. Doolittle found himself pressed into service as a test pilot, providing Laird's mechanics with detailed written critiques of the problems. Together they had worked near-miracles with the little ship by the time Doolittle flew it to Burbank, California, for the first Bendix race in 1931.

The run to Cleveland for a prize of $7,500 was no contest: The Laird biplane with its supercharged, 535-horsepower Wasp Jr. radial engine was clearly superior to the other entrants from the moment Doolittle climbed almost vertically for altitude and howled eastward toward San Bernardino Pass. He held the Laird at exactly 11,000 feet—not 50 feet higher or 50 feet lower—as he crossed the coastal mountains and then gained speed in a long, flat descent in which he lost precisely 100 feet in every four miles while crossing the Arizona deserts.

Special crews filled his tanks in just seven minutes at Albuquerque and got him airborne almost as quickly at Kansas City. He picked up a tail wind by veering slightly to the south and was doing 240 miles per hour as he tore across the finish line at Cleveland more than 60 minutes ahead of his closest pursuer. But his day was not over. Bendix was offering an additional $2,500 to the pilot who broke Frank Hawks's transcontinental record. Doolittle taxied up to a gasoline truck and

In the Gee Bee R-1, Doolittle hurtles to a land speed record of 296 mph in 1932. "I gave her the gun," he said, "and she flew like a bullet."

climbed out of his cockpit to seize the nozzle of its fueling hose as soon as his wheels stopped rolling at Cleveland. But when he headed east once more, as *The New York Times* reported, "his troubles started."

The sky blackened. "Pelting rain stung him so that he had to cower behind the cowling of the cockpit and fly by instrument." But Doolittle turned aside for nothing. He came over the airport at Newark in a diving circle, tore around its perimeter at 275 miles per hour and touched his wheels down at 4:51:10 p.m.—1 hour 8 minutes 53 seconds faster than the existing record.

Rain had eaten away the protective covering on the leading edges of the plane's wings, and parts of the cowling had been torn by the wind. For a few minutes after landing, Doolittle was dazed by carbon monoxide fumes that had leaked into his cockpit. He had subsisted on one glass of water, taken at Albuquerque, but according to a reporter he refused food, hastened work on his plane as if the record were still to be broken, and in a half hour—in a hurry to rejoin his family in Cleveland—he disappeared again to the west. He broke his west-east time by 20 minutes on the return to Cleveland and had flown 2,882 miles in all when he climbed out of the *Super Solution* at the end of the day.

Doolittle intended to enter the Bendix cross-country race and the Thompson speed contest at the National Air Races of 1932 (a broken piston had forced him out of the Thompson race in 1931). Four days before the Bendix he went to Wichita, Kansas, to test improvements Laird had made on his plane: a more powerful radial engine to increase speed and a retractable undercarriage to reduce drag. The engine ran well and the landing gear retracted as planned. But the wheels would not go back into position for landing and Doolittle had to belly-land, damaging his racer beyond any hope of competing that year.

News of his misfortune reached Zantford Granville of the Granville brothers, builders of the Gee Bee racers in Springfield, Massachusetts. Russell Boardman, who had been scheduled to fly a new Gee Bee in the upcoming Thompson Trophy race, had been injured in a crash and Granville asked Doolittle to take his place.

Doolittle jumped at the chance but was startled by the appearance of the Gee Bee when he arrived at Springfield. The plane's huge, cowled radial engine, its stubby, barrel-shaped fuselage and tiny vertical fin strongly suggested the instability that was to prove the undoing of many good men. But these characteristics bespoke brute power and raw speed as well, and Doolittle was fascinated as he examined the plane foot by foot. He climbed in, started the engine and, when asked by Granville where he was going, yelled, "Cleveland, of course!"

Doolittle called it "the touchiest plane I had ever been in." When he took it up at Cleveland to practice pylon turns, he climbed to 5,000 feet instead of the normal racing altitude of 250 feet or lower, and reported later, "It's a good thing I did. That airplane did two snap rolls before I could get it under control. Had I practiced that near the ground I would

Wreathed in flowers, Doolittle's Gee Bee R-1 is paraded like a victorious race horse before the stands at Cleveland after finishing first in the 1932 Thompson. Asked years later how he flew the tricky plane, Doolittle replied: "Very carefully."

have been dead." But he soon knew the airplane well enough to set a new world speed record in the qualifying runs, averaging 296.287 miles per hour (and hitting 309.040 miles per hour on his fastest run).

By race day in September, he had worked out a strategy. He would use the craft's power and the leverage of its variable pitch propeller to seize the lead at takeoff and fly wide of the three pylons—his throttle wide open—to maintain speed and to avoid having to bank sharply on the turns. The Thompson contest included the hottest pilots and planes in racing: Jimmy Wedell, Roscoe Turner and Jimmy Haizlip in Wedell-Williams Specials, Lee Gehlbach in a *Gee Bee R-2* (sister ship to Doolittle's R-1), and Ray Moore in builder Keith Rider's *San Francisco I.*

Doolittle got off to the fast start he wanted and increased his lead so steadily that he lapped every contestant except Wedell. He was so far ahead of the field at the finish that his victory seemed easy to laymen. But his fellow aviators knew better. They saw his performance in the Thompson as a rare feat of airmanship by a flier of unusual courage and skill—a view that was confirmed later as the temperamental Gee Bees began maiming and killing their pilots.

Doolittle reacted prudently to his success. He retired from racing a few weeks later, his experience with the plane—which was now being called the "flying death trap"—having convinced him that the cost of air racing in lives and equipment had grown too high.

Doolittle's decision came after he had met racing's ultimate challenges by winning the Bendix and Thompson Trophies, and at a time when he was in demand in other areas of aviation as salesman, engineer and pilot. His irrepressible colleague, Roscoe Turner, on the other hand, had no such victories, no such options and, having struggled into the limelight with his lion cub, still burned to prove himself the greatest as well as the best-dressed racing pilot of all time.

The National Air Races of 1933 were in many ways typical of the triumphs, disasters and financial setbacks Turner would experience in pursuit of that goal. The races were headquartered in Los Angeles that year, with the Bendix starting from Floyd Bennett Field in New York. As race time approached, Turner, flirting with bankruptcy as usual, eluded a process server by wearing grubby overalls over his dashing uniform and carrying a wrench everywhere he went.

Turner had mounted a more powerful Wasp engine on the Wedell-Williams racer he had flown to third place in the 1932 Bendix and Thompson races. Although it gulped an unheard-of 75 gallons of gas per hour and forced him to make an extra refueling stop, he led the field across country to an easy victory in the Bendix, climaxed by a dazzling display of aerobatics above Los Angeles Municipal Airport.

It was the same story—Turner out in front—a few days later in the Thompson Trophy speed race, until Turner cut inside a pylon on the first lap, when all six planes in the race were bunched together. Deciding it would be too dangerous to circle the pylon again in the path of the other contestants, Turner waited until they had thinned out and made up the turn on the second lap. But an official disqualified him because he had failed to make up the turn immediately, as the rules required. Denied a clean sweep of the major trophies by a technicality, Turner could only wait for next year.

But he was immobilized in California with a leaking fuel tank when the rest of the field took off for Cleveland in the 1934 Bendix. After only two aircraft managed to finish the race, Vincent Bendix tried to compensate for the lackluster contest by offering a $3,500 prize to anyone who could break the transcontinental speed record—which Turner had set in 1933. Turner promptly took off from Los Angeles in weather so foul that no other pilot would brave it. He electrified a huge crowd in Cleveland by materializing there amid a deluge of rain after beating the time of the previous day's Bendix winner, Doug Davis, by more than an hour. He cursed steadily under his breath as mechanics wasted precious minutes trying to push an ill-fitting funnel into his tank, but he was finally re-

A Dutch DC-2, stuck on a soggy runway near Darwin, gets help from spectators on its way to second place in the MacRobertson Race.

An adventurous outing to Australia

In 1934, twenty planes from seven countries set off on the longest air race the world had seen—11,323 miles from Mildenhall, England, to Melbourne, Australia. The MacRobertson Race, named for an Australian, Sir MacPherson Robertson, who put up a $60,000 purse, followed a course across 21 countries and posed an unprecedented challenge to aircraft endurance and pilot skills.

Nine planes reached Melbourne, the winner, a de Havilland Comet, in just under 71 hours—one third the time of previous flights. The race demonstrated to a fascinated world the new capabilities of aviation. "Truly," said a Melbourne paper, "we live in wondrous times."

Winning pilots C. W. A. Scott and T. Campbell Black of England parade in Melbourne.

fueled, roared away into the storm and got to Long Island's Floyd Bennett Field, breaking his own record by 2 minutes 39 seconds. Still, he had missed the Bendix, and although there was still the Thompson race, there again could be no clean sweep for Turner in 1934.

Fifty-five thousand people watched the start of the Thompson and it looked as though Turner would again be denied a victory. Doug Davis, also in a Wedell-Williams, held the lead for the first half of the 10-lap race despite everything the second-place Turner tried. Then, on the eighth lap, Davis missed a pylon and pulled up sharply to try again. He put his aircraft into a high speed stall, slammed into the ground with terrific force and was killed instantly. It was a somber Turner who accepted the acclaim he had sought for five years, becoming the only pilot besides Doolittle to win both the Bendix and the Thompson. His financial problems persisted, however, and the nature of his victories seemed to deny him the unqualified recognition for which he thirsted.

Turner had the fastest airplane in the race and was the heavy favorite as the field took off from Burbank early on the morning of August 30, to begin the 1935 renewal of the Bendix. But Benny Howard and his copilot Gordon Israel used the features they had designed into their high-winged racer, *Mister Mulligan,* to challenge him. The increased range of their aircraft eliminated all but one refueling stop (Turner made three) and its higher ceiling enabled them to get on top of storms that slowed the rest of the contestants.

Turner punched through the rain clouds over Cleveland and flashed across the finish line 23.5 seconds short of *Mister Mulligan's* time. It was learned later that generosity had done him in: He had insisted that a competing pilot refuel first from the single gas truck at Kansas City.

It was Turner's last try for the Bendix Trophy, as it turned out. And had it not been for his incredible reflexes and airmanship, the Thompson race a few days later in 1935 would have been his last flight ever.

"The famous Thompson Trophy race had been a great bore for eight of the ten laps," wrote columnist Paul Gallico, when Turner's Wedell-Williams "suddenly gave forth a great puff of coal black smoke." Its supercharger had disintegrated and scalding oil was spurting from the wounded engine. "The tin voice of the public address system yelled, 'Turner is in trouble . . .' The crowd let out a groan and Turner pulled the ship straight up into the air so you could see its golden belly. Up and up went Turner, fighting for the airman's salvation—altitude. They fly that Thompson race 50 to 250 feet above the ground. Your only hope is to get yourself a thousand and bail out."

Turner chose another course. He yanked his ship around after going over in a chandelle and headed back to the field. "He came in apouring," Gallico wrote, "snicked the switch, bounced once, hung, hit at terrific speed, and then was safe, rolling along the ground, the red fire wagon coming along at an angle to meet him. Always the perfect showman, he brought his dead, fuming ship to a stop, his wheels *exactly* touching the white chalk line in front of the grandstand."

The sides of Turner's plane and his face were black with oil, but his boots and tunic were immaculate. The crowd roared a welcome and he raised both hands as though embracing them. As he stepped shakily away from his bruised, but intact, airplane, a bystander expressed sympathy for his bad luck. "When something like that happens and you walk away from it," shot back Turner, "that's good luck."

Turner's typically desperate financial situation had been part of his motivation, he admitted later, for not bailing out. By the next year he was in even deeper financial trouble and he looked to prize money from the National Air Races, being held in Los Angeles again in 1936, to bail him out. As he took off from Glendale, California, to fly to New York for the start of the Bendix race, his prospects seemed excellent.

Not for long. His engine failed over New Mexico. He managed a rough but reasonable landing and had things under control until the aircraft ran onto a freshly plowed field, cartwheeled and was demolished. The doctors who looked him over diagnosed "two cracked ribs and a very short temper." He was out of the race and out of money.

A lesser man might have bowed to the dictates of fate and given up. But Turner had the wreckage of the Wedell-Williams shipped back to California, and set out to create a superplane of his own. He talked two professors of aeronautical engineering—John D. Akerman and Howard W. Barlow of the University of Minnesota—into translating his rough but strongly held ideas (he talked vaguely of "thin wings") into a set of detailed technical drawings. He sent the plans to Lawrence Brown, owner of a small Los Angeles aircraft company, to be converted into reality. But Brown and Dan Halloway, his chief engineer, were appalled when they saw the blueprints, which called for a thin, stubby wing and seven separate fuel tanks connected by a nightmarish tangle of plumbing. Brown refused to follow the plans, and Turner reluctantly agreed to some changes. Brown lengthened the fuselage, redesigned the tail surfaces and engine mount, and recommended a change in the wing design. When Turner—lured out West to be photographed with his new creation—saw what Brown and Halloway had wrought, he reacted by hacking at the new plane with an ax. Brown, in turn, discovered that his client was broke. Construction stopped.

Turner next tried Matty Laird, creator of the famed *Super Solution,* at Laird's factory in Chicago. Without discussing the fact that he was characteristically out of money, he confided that Brown was building him a new racing plane but was disagreeing as to "details." Would Laird finish the job? Would he also rebuild Turner's Wedell-Williams if the wreckage was shipped East? And could he have both planes in shape for the National Air Races? It could all be done, said Laird, if his workmen were given extra pay and his engineers were given a free hand. Laird quoted a price that made Turner swallow hard. But he smiled his most dazzling smile and shook hands.

The Air Races of 1937 were only 90 days away when the wreckage of the Wedell-Williams and the components of the new racer arrived in

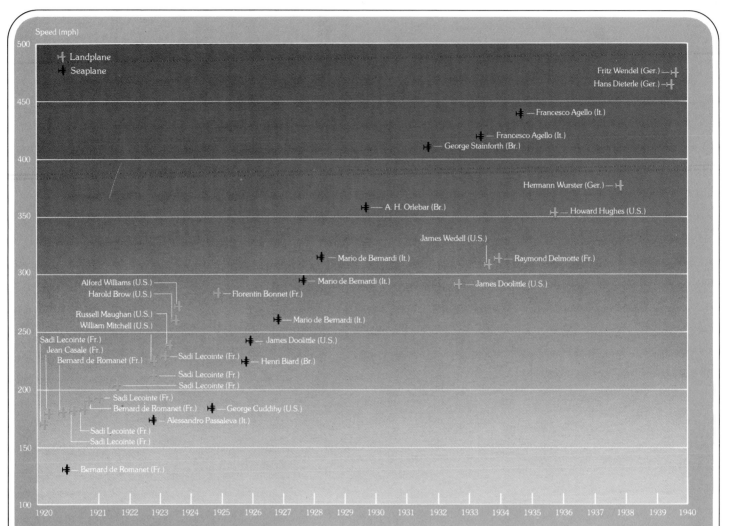

Speed (mph)

+ Landplane
+ Seaplane

Fritz Wendel (Ger.) — +
Hans Dieterle (Ger.) — +

+ — Francesco Agello (It.)

+ — Francesco Agello (It.)
+ — George Stainforth (Br.)

Hermann Wurster (Ger.) — +

+ — A. H. Orlebar (Br.)
+ — Howard Hughes (U.S.)

James Wedell (U.S.)
+ — Mario de Bernardi (It.)
+ + — Raymond Delmotte (Fr.)

Alford Williams (U.S.) —
+ — Mario de Bernardi (It.)
+ — James Doolittle (U.S.)

Harold Brow (U.S.) —
+ — Florentin Bonnet (Fr.)

Russell Maughan (U.S.) —
William Mitchell (U.S.) —
+ — Mario de Bernardi (It.)

Sadi Lecointe (Fr.)
Jean Casale (Fr.)
+ — James Doolittle (U.S.)

Bernard de Romanet (Fr.)
— Sadi Lecointe (Fr.)
+ — Henri Biard (Br.)

— Sadi Lecointe (Fr.)
— Sadi Lecointe (Fr.)

— Sadi Lecointe (Fr.)
— Bernard de Romanet (Fr.)
+ — George Cuddihy (U.S.)
+ — Alessandro Passaleva (It.)

Sadi Lecointe (Fr.)
Sadi Lecointe (Fr.)

+ — Bernard de Romanet (Fr.)

500 · 450 · 400 · 350 · 300 · 250 · 200 · 150 · 100

1920 1921 1922 1923 1924 1925 1926 1927 1928 1929 1930 1931 1932 1933 1934 1935 1936 1937 1938 1939 1940

Tracking the record

The quest for speed in flight led to dramatic increases in the world speed record during the 20 years covered by the graph above. And landplanes did not always lead the way—largely because seaplanes' longer takeoff and landing areas permitted them to use smaller wings that created less drag.

In spite of the achievements of landplane pilots like Howard Hughes *(right),* seaplanes held the speed record until it fell to a Heinkel, then a Messerschmitt, as Germany geared up for World War II.

Plane manufacturer Howard Hughes climbs from his H-1 Special, in which he set a landplane record of 352 mph in 1935.

Chicago. But in 80 days Laird had restored the Wedell-Williams to mint condition and had produced a gleaming new racing monoplane from the jumble of parts provided.

Turner talked Laird into releasing the planes without full payment by assuring the builder that he was going to win both the Bendix and Thompson races and that a pilot named Joe Mackey was going to place second in each with the Wedell-Williams. He would soon, he promised, have prize money to burn. Laird, having no real alternative, agreed, and Turner disappeared into the Western sky.

But Turner could not so easily outrun misfortune. On the eve of the Bendix race a welder making a minor repair blew up a fuel tank, taking Turner and the magnificient new plane out of the competition. Joe Mackey was forced out of the race at St. Louis. Turner—his plane repaired—led the field for a time in the Thompson, but fell to third place when he turned back to recircle a pylon he incorrectly believed he had missed. Having agreed to split his winnings with Mackey, he came away with only $1,500. Turner was horrified to think of the ease with which his creditors might now seize the new plane. He flew it in an air show in Cincinnati to earn some quick cash—then hid it under canvas in a friend's hangar there to frustrate the process servers.

Soured by misfortune, Turner doggedly arranged for a new sponsor and began the modifications calculated to bring him back to center stage. He prepared for the Thompson Trophy race of 1938 as though his life depended on it—and his financial life did. His aircraft had been designed to compete in both the Bendix and Thompson races. But in 1938 aircraft entered in one race were barred from the other because of the danger of flying the high-powered, temperamental racers across country and entering the larger, less maneuverable long-distance ships in the closed-course speed race. Turner decided to bet all on the closed-circuit race, not only because of his growing obsession with it but also because first prize had been increased to $18,000. He had the big engine tuned for low-level flight, ordered the oil cooler relocated, the navigation lights removed and the undercarriage streamlined to reduce drag. A friend flew him around and around the course at Cleveland while he memorized the location of every tree, house, field and barn he might use to guide him in the race.

In a later article titled, "Air Racing is Hell," Turner described the start of the 1938 Thompson. "My ship is ready. My hands sweat on the stick. I can't control my feet. My leg muscles are making them jump up and down on the rudder pedals. I swear as those legs keep jittering, as the clock stops, as I think of my debts, as I look ahead, fly that course in my mind. Hell! This can't go on."

Earl Ortman beat Turner off the ground, beat him to the first pylon and stayed ahead of him during the first six of 30 ten-mile laps around Cleveland's triangular course, but did so only by forcing his Marcoux-Bromberg engine to exceed the limits of its power. Turner—flying wide on the turns to avoid cutting inside a pylon—was rewarded on the

September's champions

Some of the best pilots of the 1930s never won a Thompson or Bendix race. Other fliers came tantalizingly close but failed: Earl Ortman came in second in the Bendix once and three times in the Thompson. Nonetheless, the two races—held with a few exceptions every September—set the standards of excellence in racing, benchmarks by which the public judged pilots, and the pilots judged themselves.

The winners of the prewar decade are identified here—the Thompson winners in the top two rows and the Bendix winners below—with the planes each flew and their winning speeds. Most of the victors were men, though in 1936 Louise Thaden stunned the air-racing world by becoming the first woman to win either contest—a breakthrough repeated two years later by Jacqueline Cochran.

Of widely different backgrounds, the winners varied in age (29 to 43), in physique (from Turner's burly six feet one inch to Jimmy Haizlip's four feet eleven inches in high-heeled flying boots) and in temperament: Benny Howard was mercurial and endlessly inventive, Frank Fuller as coolly incisive as a business executive—which, in fact, he was.

For all their differences, they shared exceptional skills and a willingness to take exceptional risks: Fully a third of them died pursuing their racing careers.

1930: CHARLES HOLMAN
Laird Solution
201.91 mph

1931: LOWELL BAYLES
Gee Bee Model Z
236.23 mph

1936: MICHEL DETROYAT
Caudron C-460
264.26 mph

1937: RUDY KLING
Folkerts SK-3 Jupiter
256.91 mph

1931: JAMES DOOLITTLE
Laird Super Solution
223.03 mph

1932: JAMES HAIZLIP
Wedell-Williams 92
245.00 mph

1937: FRANK FULLER
Seversky SEV-S2
258.24 mph

1938: JACQUELINE COCHRAN
Seversky SEV-S2
249.74 mph

1932: JAMES DOOLITTLE
Gee Bee R-1
252.68 mph

1933: JAMES WEDELL
Wedell-Williams 44
237.95 mph

1934: ROSCOE TURNER
Wedell-Williams 57
248.12 mph

1935: HAROLD NEUMANN
Howard Mister Mulligan
220.19 mph

1938: ROSCOE TURNER
Laird-Turner LTR-14
283.41 mph

1939: ROSCOE TURNER
Laird-Turner LTR-14
282.53 mph

1933: ROSCOE TURNER
Wedell-Williams 57
214.78 mph

1934: DOUGLAS DAVIS
Wedell-Williams 44
216.23 mph

1935: BENJAMIN HOWARD
Howard Mister Mulligan
238.70 mph

1936: LOUISE THADEN
Beechcraft C-17R
165.34 mph

1939: FRANK FULLER
Seversky SEV-S2
282.09 mph

A *flower-bedecked Roscoe Turner accepts the Thompson Trophy in 1939 from race promoter Cliff Henderson (far left) and Fred Crawford, president*

of the sponsoring Thompson company.

seventh lap when Ortman's engine began emitting a thin trail of black smoke. Turner swept into the lead—counting laps by yanking strips of masking tape from his instrument panel each time the grandstands came into view—and stayed there, finishing a full lap ahead of the field.

Thunderous applause, the sound he had waited so long to hear, again followed Turner as he walked to the judge's stand, where he was not only handed the huge Thompson Trophy for the second time—thus becoming unique among racing pilots—but was released at last from the humiliation of constant debt. He received checks for $22,000, having won an extra $4,000 for breaking the course record with an average speed of 283.42 miles per hour. He paid his creditors (though he was so irritated with the credit being given them for the success of his plane he sent not another nickel to Laird or Brown) and breathed easily once more in his self-appointed role as hero of the American skies.

He played the part to the hilt while winning the Thompson Trophy race a third time in 1939 (an event that was overshadowed two days earlier by the declaration of war on Germany by Britain and France). Once again, he cut a pylon on the very first lap, and was in last place by the time he circled it again. Then he poured it on, pushing his 14-cylinder Twin Wasp beyond its rated limits, and by the ninth circuit he was in first place and had lapped the entire field. Still, he risked his engine, his ship and his neck to achieve speeds approaching 400 miles per hour and to lap the field a second time before crossing the finish line.

He landed to accept the $16,000 winner's purse and the applause he craved—and to resign from air racing forever. "Make room for the photographers," he shouted from the cockpit. "It's their last chance to shoot me in the Thompson. Pylon racing is a young man's game. I am 43."

Fate not only enlarged the legends created in the 1930s by Turner and Doolittle but provided both with happy endings. Turner became a prosperous member of the aviation establishment; Doolittle the most celebrated Air Force general of World War II. They left behind them an era in aviation that had begun before World War I with Lincoln Beachey and the exhibition fliers, had been dramatized by the barnstormers and aerial circuses of the 1920s and had reached its zenith before hundreds of thousands of people at the National Air Races of the 1920s and 1930s. The whole brave phenomenon was interrupted rudely by World War II and was swallowed forever by the technological changes prompted by that war. With it vanished a quality of mind and a quality of life—a certain innocence, a reckless individualism.

The men and women who flew the Jennies and later the *Gee Bees*, the *Super Solution* and the Wedell-Williams racers were direct descendants and, in many ways, the final heirs of the footloose frontiersmen of an earlier century who had crossed the Appalachians and wandered the West; they risked their lives as a matter of course because that was the only way to reach the next mountain range—or to achieve the next aerial stunt—and the prize still seems worth the gamble. ➳

Acknowledgments

The index for this book was prepared by Gale Linck Partoyan. For their help in the preparation of this book, the editors wish to thank John Amendola, artist *(pages 26-27, 132-139),* Frederic F. Bigio, artist *(page 166)* and John Young, artist *(endpaper and cover detail, regular edition).* For their valuable help with the preparation of this volume, the editors wish to thank: **In Canada:** Ottawa—Joy Houston, Public Archives of Canada. **In France:** Paris—Gérard Baschet, Éditions de l'*Illustration;* Marianne de Fleury, Musée du Cinéma Henri Langlois; André Bénard, Odile Benoist, Elizabeth Caquot, Alain Degardin, Georges Delaleau, Gilbert Deloizy, Général Paul Dompnier, Deputy Director, Yvan Kayser, Général Pierre Lissarague, Director, Stéphane Nicolaou, Musée de l'Air; Edmond Petit, Curator, Musée Air-France. **In Great Britain:** Falmouth—W. E. Chapman; Hemel Hempstead—Olive French; Keighley—F. E. Draycott; London—Steve Piercey, Flight International; A. C. Harold, D. I. Roberts, Royal Air Force Museum; Marjorie Willis, BBC Hulton Picture Library; St. Albans—Harold Wilson. **In Italy:** Milan—Giorgio Apostolo, Managing Editor, *Aerofan;* Andrea Artoni, Macchi; Alfredo Hummel, Publifoto; Alberto Menozzi, Siai Marchetti; Maurizio Pagliano, Rizzoli; Rome—Countess Maria Fede Caproni, Museo Aeronautico Caproni di Taliedo; Fiorenza de Bernardi; Colonel Roberto Gasperini, Stato Maggiore Aeronautica; Turin—Augusto Costantino, Director, Centro Storico, Fiat. **In Spain:** Barcelona—Juan José Fernandez Toca, Aeroclub de Barcelona-Sabadell; Madrid—Felipe Ezquerra; Captain

Enrique Alvarez Novo; Captain Ramón Hidalgo Salazar. **In the United States:** Arizona—Jessie O. Dockery; California—Walter M. Cary; Lieutenant General James H. Doolittle USAF (Ret.); Don Dwiggins; James Haizlip; Mary Haizlip; David Hatfield, Northrop University; Clifford Henderson; Anthony Levier; Art Ronnie; Neta Southern; John Underwood; Harold Wilson, Planes of Fame Museum; Connecticut—Everett Cassagneres, Ryan Aircraft; Robert H. Stepanek, Bradley Air Museum; Beatrice LaFlamme, Harvey Lippincott, United Technologies Corporation; Washington, D.C.—Phil Edwards, Pete Suthard, Robert van der Linden, National Air and Space Museum; Michael Monroney; Arthur Renstrom, Library of Congress; Florida—Robert Elliott, George W. Haldeman, Joseph James, Roger Don Rae, Clem Whittenbeck, Paul Whittenbeck, Captain J. E. Wood, Retired Eastern Pilots Association; Jessie Woods; Illinois—Nick P. Rezich; Truman C. Weaver, Major USAF (Ret.); Iowa—E. D. Weeks; Kansas—Harold E. Neumann; Louisiana—F. C. Felterman; Jim Pitts, The *Times*-Picayune Publishing Corporation; Massachusetts—Deborah Cozort, Massachusetts Institute of Technology; Robert T. Staron, Springfield Science Museum; Eugene Zepp, Boston Public Library; Nevada—Phillip I. Earl, Nevada Historical Society; New Mexico—Harry Davidson; New York—Michaelene Carpenter; Elizabeth B. Mason, Director, Columbia University Oral History Research Office; Irving Rosenberg; Ohio—William J. Allen, Western Reserve Aviation Hall of Fame; Sidney H. Bradd; Roger Hubbell; Milan Kusenda; Kathy Louie,

Western Reserve Historical Society; M. C. Murphy; Rudy Profant, American Air Racing Society; Charles Tracy, The Cleveland Press; Oklahoma—Linda Stone, Woolaroc Museum; Oregon—Walt Bohrer; Dorothy Hester Stenzil; South Carolina—Robert Hall; Dexter C. Martin; Tennessee—John L. Parrish, Mattie Schultz, Staggerwing Museum Foundation, Inc.; Texas—Mitch Mayborn, Flying Enterprise Publications; Edward G. Rice, History of Aviation Collection, University of Texas at Dallas; Virginia—Dana Bell, U.S. Air Force Photo Depository; Vincent Burnett; Don Erskine, Bendix Aerospace Electronics; Washington—Peter M. Bowers, The Boeing Company; Wisconsin—Gene R. Chase, Experimental Aircraft Association Air Museum; Steve J. Wittman; Wyoming—Emmett D. Chisum, Transportation History Foundation, University of Wyoming. **In West Germany:** Koblenz—Marianne Loenartz, Meinrad Nilges, Bundesarchiv Koblenz; Munich—Ulrich Frodien, Süddeutscher Verlag; Herbert Studtrucker, Deutsches Museum; West Berlin—Roland Klemig, Heidi Klein, Bildarchiv Preussischer Kulturbesitz; Axel Schulz, Ullstein Bilderdienst.

Particularly useful sources of information and quotations used in this volume were: *The Schneider Trophy Races* by Ralph Barker, Chatto and Windus, 1972; *Cornwall Aviation Company* by Ted Chapman, Glasney Press, 1979; *Locklear: The Man Who Walked on Wings* by Art Ronnie, A. S. Barnes, 1973; *Old Soggy No. 1: The Uninhibited Story of Slats Rodgers* by Hart Stilwell and Slats Rodgers, Arno Press, 1972.

Bibliography

Allard, Noel, *Speed: The Biography of Charles W. Holman.* Noel E. Allard, 1976.

American Heritage, *History of Flight.* Simon & Schuster, 1962.

Angelucci, Enzo, and Paolo Matricardi, *World Aircraft: Origins—World War I.* Rand McNally, 1979.

Barker, Ralph, *The Schneider Trophy Races.* London: Chatto and Windus, 1972.

Caidin, Martin, *Barnstorming.* Duell, Sloan and Pearce, 1965.

Chapman, Ted, *Cornwall Aviation Company.* Falmouth: Glasney Press, 1979.

Cleveland, Carl M., *"Upside-Down" Pangborn: King of the Barnstormers.* Aviation Book Company, 1978.

Cobham, Sir Alan J., *A Time to Fly.* London: Shepheard-Walwyn, 1978.

Duncan, Captain Richard M. C., *Stunt Flying.* The Goodheart-Willcox Co., 1930.

Dwiggins, Don:
  The Air Devils. Grosset & Dunlap, 1966.
  The Barnstormers: Flying Daredevils of the Roaring Twenties. Grosset & Dunlap, 1968.
  They Flew the Bendix Race: The History of the Competition for the Bendix Trophy. J. B. Lippincott, 1965.

Fleischer, Suri, and Arleen Keylin, eds., *Flight As Reported by the New York Times.* Arno Press, 1977.

Foxworth, Thomas G., *The Speed Seekers.* Doubleday, 1974.

Glines, Carroll V., *Jimmy Doolittle: Daredevil Aviator and Scientist.* Macmillan, 1972.

Goldberg, Alfred, ed., *A History of the United States Air Force.* Arno Press, 1974.

Grace, Dick:
  I Am Still Alive. Rand McNally, 1931.
  Squadron of Death: The True Adventures of a Movie Plane-Crasher. Doubleday, Doran, 1929.

Harris, Sherwood, *The First to Fly: Aviation's Pioneer Days.* Simon and Schuster, 1970.

Hatfield, D. D.:
  Los Angeles Aeronautics 1920-1929. Northrop University Press, 1976.
  Aeroplane Scrapbook No. 1. Northrop University Press, 1976.

Hawks, Ellison, *British Seaplanes Triumph in the International Schneider Trophy Contests 1913-1931.* Southport, England: Real Photographs Co. Ltd., 1945.

Kinert, Reed, *Racing Planes and Air Races: A Complete History:*
  Vol. 1, *1909-1923.* Aero Publishers, 1969.
  Vol. 2, *1924-1931.* Aero Publishers, 1969.
  Vol. 3, *1932-1939.* Aero Publishers, 1969.

Komons, Nick A., *Bonfires to Beacons: Federal Civil Aviation Policy under the Air Commerce Act 1926-1938.* U.S. Department of Transportation, 1978.

Lewis, Peter, *British Racing and Record Breaking.* Putnam, 1970.

Lincke, Jack R., *Jenny Was No Lady: The Story of The JN-4D.* W. W. Norton, 1970.

Lockheed Aircraft Corporation, *Lockheed's Family Tree: A History of the Company's Early Aircraft.* Lockheed Aircraft Corporation, 1978.

Mandrake, Charles:
  National Air Races 1932. Speed Publishing, 1976.
  The Gee Bee Story. Robert R. Longo, 1956.

Munson, Kenneth:
  Flying Boats and Seaplanes Since 1910. Macmillan, 1971.
  Pioneer Aircraft 1903-1914. Macmillan, 1969.

Orlebar, A. H., *Schneider Trophy: A Personal Account of High-Speed Flying & the Winning of the Schneider Trophy.* London: Seeley Service & Co. Limited, 1929.

Reynolds, Quentin, *The Amazing Mr. Doolittle: A Biography of Lieutenant General James H. Doolittle.* Appleton-Century-Crofts, 1953.

Rhode, Bill, *Baling Wire, Chewing Gum, and Guts: The Story of the Gates Flying Circus.* Kennikat Press, 1970.

Rocchi, Renato, *La Meravigliosa Avventura.* Rome: Stato Maggiore Aeronautica, 1976.

Ronnie, Art, *Locklear: The Man Who Walked on Wings.* A. S. Barnes, 1973.

Roseberry, C. R.:
  The Challenging Skies: The Colorful Story of Aviation's Most Exciting Years, 1919-1939. Doubleday, 1966.
  Glenn Curtiss: Pioneer of Flight. Doubleday, 1972.

Rust, Kenn C., ed., *Historical Aviation Album: All American Series,* Vols. 10, 12, 13 and 14. Historical Aviation Album, 1971.

Schmid, S. H., and Major Truman C. Weaver, *Golden Age of Air Racing Pre 1940.* EAA Air Museum Foundation, Inc., 1963.

Stilwell, Hart, and Slats Rodgers, *Old Soggy No. 1: The Uninhibited Story of Slats Rodgers.* Arno Press, 1972.

Taylor, John W. R., and Kenneth Munson, *History of Aviation.* Crown Publishers, 1977.

Taylor, John W. R., Michael J. H. Taylor and David Mondey, *Air Facts & Feats.* Sterling Publishing Co., 1978.

Thomas, Lowell, and Edward Jablonski, *Doolittle: A Biography.* Doubleday, 1976.

Underwood, John W.:
Acrobats in the Sky. Heritage Press, 1972.
Monocoupes and Men. Heritage Press, 1969.

Vecsey, George, and George C. Dade, *Getting Off the Ground.* E. P. Dutton, 1979.

Vorderman, Don, *The Great Air Races.* Doubleday, 1969.

Periodicals

Aero, July 8, 1911.

"Aerobatics," *Air & Space,* December 1979.

Aero Digest, September, October 1929.

Air Travel News, October 1929.

Aviation, June 22, August 17, September 7, 1929.

"Bournemouth," *Flight,* September 6, 1929.

Boyne, Walter, "The Gee Bee Story" *Aviation Quarterly,* 2nd Quarter, 1977.

Brown, Philip C., "The Fabulous Gee Bees," *American Aviation Historical Society Journal,* Fall 1979.

"Casterline is Unhurt Sunday in Bad Mishap." *The Hartford City* (Indiana) *News,* October 17, 1928.

Elliott, Robert G., "A Silver Eagle in Retirement," *Vintage Airplane,* July-August 1974; February 1975; July-August 1976.

Forden, Lesley N., "The Dole Race," *American Aviation Historical Society Journal,* Fall 1975, Winter 1975.

Grace, Dick, "Fall Guys," *The Saturday Evening Post,* April 6, 1929.

Granville, Robert, *Sport Aviation,* December 1976; February, December 1977.

Granville, Thomas, *Sport Aviation,* March, May 1977.

"Hampton Roads," *Flight,* September 6, 1929.

Hardie, George, Jr., "Lowell R. Bayles, Race Pilot," *Sport Aviation,* January 1975.

Hasskard, R. A., "The Meteor Man," *Aerospace Historian,* August 1967.

Hay, T. Benson, "Go-Grease Benny Howard," *The Saturday Evening Post,* September 2, 1939.

James, Joseph R.:
"Gates Flying Circus," *Vintage Airplane,* August 1976.
Gates Flying Circus articles in *Popular Aviation:* May, June, July, November 1936; January, November 1937.

"King's Cup Race," *Flight,* September 14, 1922; July 19, 1923; July 9, 1925; July 15, 1926; July 11, 1929.

Lowe, Thomas, "Flying Aces Air Circus," *American Aviation Historical Society Journal,* Summer 1977.

Marshall, R. C. "Tex," "The Saga of Tex Marshall," *Western Flying,* October, November, December 1933.

"Miami All-American Air Races," *Aero Digest,* February 1931.

"Mildenhall to Melbourne," *Time,* October 29, 1924.

"On the Schneider Picnic," *The Aeroplane,* September 17, 1919.

Ord-Hume, Arthur, "The Savage Skywriters," *Aeroplane Monthly,* March 1974.

Raleigh, Walter, "Frank Hawks—the Record Breaker," *Popular Aviation,* June 1931.

Reinhardt, Charles Gilbert, "Gypsying the Jennies," *The Saturday Evening Post,* January 9, 1926.

"Schneider Contest," *Air and Airway,* September 1931.

Schneider Trophy Race articles in *Flight:* September 18, October 4, 1923; November 12, 1925; September 29, 1927; September 13, 1929; September 11, 18, 1931.

Sprigg, Christopher, "328 Miles Per Hour," *Popular Mechanics Magazine,* December 1929.

"Venice," *Flight,* September 6, 1929.

Wait, William, "Development of High Speed Racing," *Aviation,* August 24, 1929.

Weeks, E. D., "Lincoln Beachey's Last Ride," *American Aviation Historical Society Journal,* Summer 1961.

Picture credits

Credits from left to right are separated by semicolons, from top to bottom by dashes.

Front endpaper (and cover detail, regular edition): Painting by John Young. 6, 7: John W. Underwood Collection. 8: Clyde E. Pangborn Collection, Washington State University Libraries, Pullman, Washington. 9: Clyde E. Pangborn Collection, Washington State University Libraries, Pullman, Washington—Smithsonian Institution Photo No. 76-13078. 10, 11: UPI. 12, 13: U.S. Air Force Photo Depository. 14, 15: UPI. 16: Phillips Petroleum Company—Hatfield History of Aeronautics, Northrop Univesity. 17: Phillips Petroleum Company. 18, 19: Culver Pictures. 20: San Diego Historical Society's Title Insurance and Trust Collection. 23: Smithsonian Institution Photo No. A-4522. 24, 25: Library of Congress. 26, 27: Drawing by John Amendola Studio. 28: Brown Brothers. 29: Don Dwiggins Collection. 31: Indiana Historical Society. 32: Art Ronnie. 33: History of Aviation Collection, University of Texas at Dallas, Donation of Anita Locklear. 35: courtesy Oregon Historical Society. 38, 39: Hatfield History of Aeronautics, Northrop University. 40, 41: courtesy D. W. Phillips, Midhurst. 42, 43: courtesy D. W. Phillips, Midhurst; courtesy M. E. Adams, Hemel Hempstead—courtesy Doreen Crews, Cornwall. 44, 45: courtesy A. J. Jackson, Essex. 46: Hatfield History of Aeronautics, Northrop University. 48: Smithers Collection, Humanities Research Center, The University of Texas at Austin. 50: John W. Underwood Collection. 52: Minnesota Historical Society. 54, 55: Hatfield History of Aeronautics, Northrop University. 56, 57: courte-

sy Robert G. Elliott from Lt. Col. (Ret.) Clinton E. Herberger Collection. 58: Art Ronnie. 59: Library of Congress. 61: The Granger Collection, New York—courtesy Planes of Fame Museum; Dmitri Kessel, Musée du Cinéma Henri Langlois, Paris. 62, 63: Culver Pictures. 65: Hatfield History of Aeronautics, Northrop University. 66: courtesy Jessie Woods. 68, 69: Smithsonian Institution Photo No. 80-13753. 70, 71: Wide World. 72, 73: Bradd Collection. 74, 75: Éditions de l'Illustration, Paris. 76: Giancarlo Costa, Milan. 78: Musée de l'Air, Paris. 81: *Flight International,* London. 85: Musée de l'Air, Paris; *Flight International,* London; Ann Natanson, courtesy Museo Aeronautico Caproni di Taliedo, Rome—UPI; BBC Hulton Picture Library, London; The Bettmann Archive—Bradd Collection; Fiat Centro Storico, Turin; *Flight International,* London—The Bettmann Archive (2). 87: *Flight International,* London. 88, 89: courtesy The Baltimore Sunpapers. 90: *The New York Times.* 92: *Flight International,* London. 93: Museo Aeronautico Caproni de Taliedo, Rome. 94: National Archives Neg. No. 306-NT-1287-16. 96, 97: courtesy Royal Air Force Museum, Hendon. 98: National Archives Neg. No. 306-NT-168-220C. 99-101: UPI. 102, 103: Wide World; The N. Paul Whittier Historical Aviation Library-Leslie Forden Collection. 104, 105: Peter M. Bowers Collection. 106, 107: Library of Congress. 108: UPI. 110, 111: Dick Whittington. 112: Bradd Collection—Wayne Rayburn, courtesy of the Reference-Room of the Crawford Auto-Aviation Museum, Western Reserve Historical Society, Cleveland, Ohio. 113: The Granger Collec-

tion, New York; Bradd Collection (2). 115: Chicago Historical Society Neg. No. IChi-14117—Art Ronnie. 118: Derek Bayes, courtesy Science Museum, London—Henry Beville, courtesy National Air and Space Museum, Smithsonian Institution; Henry Groskinsky, courtesy National Air and Space Museum, Smithsonian Institution. 119: Henry Groskinsky, courtesy Clifford Henderson, displayed in National Air and Space Museum, Smithsonian Institution. 120-127: Bradd Collection. 128: Rudy Profant Collection. 131: UPI. 132-139: Drawings by John Amendola Studio. 140, 141: *Plain Dealer* Photo. 142, 143: courtesy of the Reference-Room of the Crawford Auto-Aviation Museum, Western Reserve Historical Society, Cleveland, Ohio. 144, 145: John W. Underwood Collection. 146, 147: Rudy Profant Collection. 148: courtesy of the Boston Public Library, Print Department. 152: Wide World. 153: Smithsonian Institution Photo No. 78-13936. 155, 156: Bradd Collection. 158, 159: UPI. 161: Bradd Collection. 163: BBC Hulton Picture Library, London—National Library of Australia, Canberra. 166: Frederic F. Bigio, B-C Graphics—Wide World. 168: Bradd Collection (4)—Bradd Collection; The Bendix Corporation—UPI (2). 169: Smithsonian Institution Photo No. 80-13450; Wide World; American Heritage Center, University of Wyoming; UPI—American Heritage Center, University of Wyoming; Smithsonian Institution Photo No. 80-13744—Bradd Collection (2); The Bendix Corporation; Smithsonian Institution Photo No. 77-4173—Rudy Profant Collection. 170, 171: Bradd Collection.

Index